Brian Barton was born in Dunkineely, Co. Donegal, in 1944, and educated at Methodist College, Belfast. He graduated from Queen's University, Belfast, in 1967, was awarded an M.A. by the University of Ulster in 1979 and a Ph.D. by Queen's University in 1986. He has taught at the Belfast Institute, and has been Research Fellow at the Institute of Irish Studies, Q.U.B., and at Churchill College, Cambridge. He is currently research fellow in the Politics Department at Queen's. He has written *Brookeborough; the Making of a Prime Minister* (Belfast, 1988), and *The Blitz; Belfast in the War Years,* (Belfast, 1989), has co-edited two volumes on contemporary Irish politics and has recently completed `Northern Ireland, 1921-1951' for *A New History of Ireland, Vol. VIII*, (Clarendon Press, forthcoming).

NORTHERN IRELAND
IN THE
SECOND WORLD WAR

BRIAN BARTON

ULSTER HISTORICAL
FOUNDATION

To Valerie, Deirdre and Allen

Cover photographs:
Front: VE Day celebrations at Belfast City Hall, courtesy *Belfast Telegraph*;
Douglas Dakota courtesy of Dermott Dunbar
Back: P38 bombers on route from docks to base passing
through the empty early morning streets, courtesy *Belfast Telegraph*

Published 1995
by the Ulster Historical Foundation
12 College Square East, Belfast, BT1 6DD

ISBN 0-901905-690

Typeset by the Ulster Historical Foundation
Printed by ColourBooks Ltd, Dublin

Cover and Design by Dunbar Design

Grateful acknowledgement for financial assistance is made to Belfast City Council,
the Milibern Trust, the Elizabeth Ellison Fund and the Cultural Traditions
Programme of the Community Relations Council which aims to encourage
acceptance and understanding of cultural diversity

CONTENTS

ACKNOWLEDGEMENTS

I wish to thank the staff of the following institutions for their assitance: The Public Record Office of Northern Ireland, Belfast; the Public Record Office, London; the Imperial War Museum, in particular C.J. Bruce; the Tom Harrisson Mass Observation Archive, especially Dorothy Sheridan; the Langford Lodge Wartime Centre; the National Archive, Dublin; the National Library of Ireland; the Archives Centre, Churchill College, Cambridge; the Main Library, Queen's University, Belfast; the Central Library, Belfast, and the Linen Hall Library, Belfast, especially John Killen and Gerry Healy.

I must also express my gratitude to the Deputy Keeper of the Records, Public Record Office of Northern Ireland, for granting me permission to quote form material deposited there. Mass Observation material is reproduced by permission of the Trustees of the Tom Harrisson Mass Observation Archive, University of Sussex. In addition, Maureen van Tiggelen was kind enough to make available papers relating to the Belgian troops based in Northern Ireland during the war.

Most sincere thanks are also due to those who provided photographs and other material with which to illustrate the text; the Belfast Telegraph, in particular David Millar and Peter Bainbridge; David Ashe and Trudy Watson of Langford Lodge Wartime Centre; Roger Strong of the Public Record Office, Northern Ireland; Ernie Cromie of the Ulster Aviation Society; Jim Mullen, Derry City Council; Dermott Dunbar; the Imperial War Museum and the Ulster Folk and Transport Museum.

I wish to express my most profound gratitude to my publishers, the Ulster Historical Foundation, whose expertise and encouragement were crucial in shaping the present volume — in particular to the professionalism of Trevor Parkhill, to Shane McAteer and to Dr Brian Trainor. I would like to thank Elizabeth Belshaw, who typset the manuscript for her promptitude, and Wendy Dunbar for providing her skill and expertise in designing the cover and lay-out of both text and illustrations.

I am also deeply grateful to Belfast City Council, the Milibern Trust, the Elizabeth Ellison Fund and the Community Relations Council for the generous financial support they have provided for this publication.

Brian Barton

Sunderland aircraft on runway, at Castle Archdale, County Fermanagh
Imperial War Museum; Ernie Cromie, Ulster Aviation Society

INTRODUCTION

Northern Ireland on the eve of war

In Fermanagh in 1918, claims were made that Enniskillen was the first town in the United Kingdom to hear of the armistice; the military barracks there picked up a faint message from France at 6:30 am, on 11 November, and conveyed the news to the county by launching a series of rockets. The imminence of a second war in Europe was transmitted a little more easily. Breege McCusker has recorded:

> The beginning of September 1939 was very warm. Many of the people of Fermanagh were busy with their last bit of farming. Joe Kane, of Drumkeeran, Ederney, remembers well the fear felt by everyone on Friday, 1 September. He was working on a neighbour's farm helping to cut the corn. There was a scarcity of wirelesses and news was difficult to get. Kitty Jones came down to the men in the field to announce that Hitler had invaded Poland. She told them that he had five cities blazing in Poland by 5 o'clock that morning ... There was a real fear of Germany felt among the locals. Many old superstitions were recalled. The absence of the robin that winter was seen as a sign that Ireland would be invaded.[1]

Meanwhile, in Belfast, there had been for several months ominous portents of the impending conflict. The *Belfast Telegraph* reported nightly queues of volunteers at the army recruitment office, Clifton Street, in late August and early September. Belfast Corporation workers were coating kerbs, lampposts, telegraph poles and trees with bands of white paint in preparation for the blackout; the primary intention was to prevent Northern Ireland being used by the enemy to identify targets in Britain. Transport vehicles were shrouded in a dull blue, and their lights dimmed; some buses were in the process of being converted into mobile casualty posts and cars into makeshift ambulances. The distribution of gas masks was being completed by wardens, most without uniforms. Trenches in parks and at schools, closed in after the Munich crisis, were being re-opened and many business premises sand-bagged against blast damage. Preparations were being made by the government to increase the capacity of hospitals, to draw up plans to evacuate the city's 70,000 schoolchildren, and to receive air-raid warnings from Britain and transmit them to the public using factory sirens. The compulsory provision of workers' shelters by factories and the corporation had been introduced but was restricted to the most vulnerable part of the city — the harbour. The government had itself distributed some free to householders beginning in certain limited areas near the danger zone. Neither the people nor their leaders had any real inkling of the likely impact of war.

Much had happened in Ireland since it last faced the prospect of conflict in Europe and beyond. The most notable political event was partition in 1921, and the formation of Northern Ireland, with its own devolved parliament and limited powers of self-government. Sir James Craig had become its first, and remained its only, Prime Minister. Early hopes of internal inter-communal harmony quickly disappeared. The north progressively became an ever more protestant state, and the catholic minority isolated, resentful and alienated. For Sir James, it seemed enough that the border, his government and a dominant united Unionist Party should survive. The prevalence of the constitutional issue and strength of sectarian feeling helped impede any socialist challenge.

Meanwhile, north-south relations became embedded in a sterile state of cold war. From the outset, a fundamental distrust existed between the two Irish governments. The Dublin leadership's refusal officially to recognise Northern Ireland caused hostility amongst Unionists. The relationship deteriorated further after Eamon de Valera became Taoiseach in February 1932; his 1937 constitution contained a constitutional and territorial claim over the six counties. At the same time, the gulf between the two states widened — the border became increasingly like a frontier. Eire's imposition of high and wide-ranging tariffs in the early 1930s disrupted cross-border trade. As the six county area became more protestant in its political and public life and fostered close links with Britain, the south became more catholic, republican and gaelic in character. De Valera stated that he would 'not tomorrow, for the sake of a united Ireland, give up the policy of trying to make this a really Irish-Ireland — not by any means'.[2]

Northern Ireland was, from its formation, the most politically divided region of the United Kingdom; in addition, by the late '30s, it had emerged as the most socially and economically disadvantaged. In early 1939, approximately 90,000 of its workers were unemployed, proportionately more than in any region in Great Britain. It had also the highest death rate; maternal mortality actually rose during the inter-war years. At the same time, its educational services fell perhaps a generation behind provision in England

and Wales. In 1944, a government enquiry would estimate that almost one third of its housing stock was in urgent need of replacement.

While Westminster contributed towards the cost of Northern Ireland's social services (e.g. its national insurance, national assistance and pension schemes), overall it treated the area less generously than regions in Britain. It was evident that many British ministers felt little real commitment to the north. A report by leading Whitehall officials said of these years that 'all political parties [were then] able to take the line over partition that there [was] nothing they would like better than to see a united Ireland.'[3] Even in 1920-21 this outcome was widely regarded at Westminster as both desirable and inevitable. It was of course anticipated that a future united Irish state would remain within the empire and would evolve peacefully without the coercion of the unionist population. This was assumed even by Labour MPs, the party which favoured Irish unity most enthusiastically.

A number of these inter-war characteristics of the province survived the second world war. In some respects, however, the conflict caused a major reversal of previous trends. The most important new development was to be the much warmer relationship between Westminster and Stormont, which developed almost unobserved during its course. This provided the foundation stone for the social and economic progress which characterised the 1950s and early '60s. It was an outcome which could not easily have been foreseen in 1939.

1
THE IMPACT OF WAR
ON NORTHERN IRELAND

The disruptive impact of war

On Sunday, 3 September 1939, at 11.15am, Neville Chamberlain informed the nation that a state of war existed between Britain and Germany. Both the sadness in his voice and his choice of words betrayed his own feelings of deep , personal grief; he had, as a biographer once said of his father, Joseph, held out the hand of friendship and it had been bitten to the bone. On the following morning, under the headline *Hitler plunges the world into war*, the *Belfast News Letter* sought to draw consolation from the fact that at least the recent interminable sequence of international crises had ended. That day (4 September) the Northern Ireland parliament met at Stormont; it had been recalled one month early from its summer recess. The spectre of war dominated its proceedings. Some MPs voiced concern that German bombers were just 2½ hours' flying time from Ulster and spoke of 'panic abroad' in the streets of Belfast. Craig's speech dominated later news coverage; it betrayed a certain unconscious remoteness from the conflict. He promised a tense and expectant Commons that there would be 'no slackening in [Ulster's] loyalty. There is no falling off in our determination to place the whole of our resources at the command of the [imperial] government ... anything we can do to facilitate them ... they have only just got to let us know.'[1]

His comments echoed the sentiments expressed by a Commons' resolution, passed on 22 March 1938 at the height of the Munich crisis. It stated that Britain could 'confidently rely upon the people of loyal Ulster to share the responsibilities and burden... to the utmost of their resources'.[2] In reality, from the early stages of the conflict, a stark and, for some local ministers, embarrassing contrast rapidly emerged between the province's wartime experience and that found elsewhere in the United Kingdom. In the six counties, attitudes, patterns of behaviour and the overall pace of life were uniquely static and unchanging. Even its official war history describes the period after the outbreak of hostilities as monotonous and a time of little progress towards victory, when inactivity persisted.

Of course, a considerable level of disruption in wartime could not be avoided and much of it was transmitted direct from Westminster; as time wore on , the impact of the conflict inevitably bit more deeply. A blackout order was imposed on 1 September 1939, and petrol rationing exactly four weeks later. National registration in October was the necessary preliminary to the rationing of food, which began in 1940 and became increasingly severe and extensive. From the spring of that year government regulations and uncertain supplies, aggravated by hoarding, gradually forced changes in the pattern of public consumption and some small traders out of business. In Belfast, shopping steadily became more time-consuming and laborious, with queues reported, even at down-town bread shops. Unfamiliar purchases had to be made. Within the first 12 months of war, down-market products such as pigs' knees, feet and cheeks made their first appearance in the shop windows of smart, city centre butchers; meat consumption overall fell sharply. Fruit — tinned or fresh — became almost unobtainable, as did dairy products such as cheese and cream. Even eggs virtually 'disappeared overnight' with the introduction of strict rationing in mid-1941. At about the same time, its extension to clothing 'killed the trade', leaving even expensive retail stores deserted. It reinforced the emerging fashion for tweeds amongst the better-off — especially those 'quieter in tone', which would not be 'remembered if worn for several years'.[3] By then, ordinary household goods, such as matches (increasingly bought by the half-dozen rather than by the box) and luxury goods — spirits, cigarettes, cosmetics and even hairclips — were difficult to find. Cumulatively, these trends sapped morale and aroused a growing sense of dread as to long-term prospects if the war continued. Ironically, on occasion more affluent consumers found that goods such as soapflakes or tinned milk were more readily available in corner shops in working-class areas than at grocers in their own districts.

There were numerous other sources of irritation experienced, especially by the better-off. Domestic servants became steadily more difficult to attract as alternative war-time occupations expanded. Moya Woodside, a surgeon's wife living in south Belfast, noted that 'anyone who has a maid at all is holding on to her like grim death'.[4] Travel was restricted. Though exit permits were not required to cross the border, triptychs were withdrawn in 1940 so that the south could only be visited by public transport — train or bus. Generally, movement to Britain was limited to those taking up war-related employment or who were on national service or who had a near relative there who was seriously ill. Petrol rationing drastically reduced road traffic within the province; beyond the immediate Belfast area, it was virtually confined to military vehicles and farm carts. Bus services ceased to operate after 6-7pm in most urban areas.

At the same time, there was a progressive narrowing and impoverishment of cultural life. Subscriptions to foreign publications had to be cancelled. Entertainers, visiting lecturers and university examiners found increasing difficulty in obtaining travel permits to cross from Britain; in any case, due to rationing, catering for them was problematical. Those from Eire were discouraged by fear of bombs and dislike of the blackout. Sources of information — newspapers and the BBC — were heavily censored. In some respects, this may have been counter-productive. It bred the widespread suspicion or anxiety that 'the bad news ... must be worse' than reported and that any 'good news' was just 'so much propaganda and/or wishful thinking'.[5] The London blitz, the incidence of strikes locally or epidemics such as scabies were ignored or under-reported. Belfast's first air-raid alert, on 26 October 1940, was virtually the sole topic of conversation in the city at the time but was barely visible in press reports being concealed behind accounts of a visit by the Duke of Kent.

Anti-aircraft Bofors gun emplacement, with crew, in Belfast; the censor's mark visible in this *Belfast Telegraph* photograph

Another major disruptive impact of war was the military invasion by allied forces which gathered pace from the early summer of 1940. Much of the north struggled to absorb the burgeoning camps occupied initially by British troops — 70,000 by November 1940, and over 100,000 by April 1941. At first many lived under canvas but later a greater proportion occupied billets, requisitioned buildings or lived in hutted quarters especially constructed for the purpose. Two waves of American forces followed from 1942-44. For much of the war personnel from all three services and from many of the anti-fascist belligerent nations and groups were represented in the six counties; they numbered over 300,000 in total. Already during the late 1940s, Belfast was described as 'jammed with officers' and their families.[6] The population of an undesignated town 30 miles away was boosted from its normal 12,500 to 18,000. In Londonderry, the number of military personnel rose from 1,000 in 1939 to a peak of 40,000 in 1943; if its neighbouring airports are included, this was roughly the equivalent of the city's population. At one point it was calculated that up to 25% of Fermanagh's population was comprised of servicemen. One local historian noted that it had not had 'so many strangers' even in 'plantation times'.[7] Throughout the county 'people found themselves in the happy position of having money in their pockets for the first time'.[8]

All over the north the military presence inflated the trade of shops, public houses, cafes and cinemas. In Fermanagh it created 'full employment for all except for the unemployable'.[9] It also resulted in increased social activity. Even the hitherto isolated, peaceful farming and fishing life of Boa Island was shattered by the khaki invasion; as a consequence its social life was described as hectic. This was especially the case for 'high society' throughout the province. In Belfast, Mrs Woodside recorded the endless round of 'sherry parties, regimental entertainments, dinners'. In attendance there was a profusion of 'red tabs, bristling moustaches, monocles, women with silver-fox furs, large red mouths and red, claw-like nails'. The final image was appropriate; canteen work as cooks, waitresses and dishwashers was, she noted, 'astonishingly popular' with well-off women from 'fashionable parts of town' who neglected homes and husbands to perform work normally delegated to maids and charwomen. She explained the attraction: 'it's our old friend SEX ... vast numbers of unattached, bored, sex-starved men in uniform', combined with the 'wartime relaxing of conventions'.[10]

The presence of such large numbers of troops also created problems. On Sundays in late 1940 'hundreds and hundreds of men in uniform' could be seen 'wandering about' Belfast with 'nothing to do and nowhere to go'. Cinemas (until 1943) and public houses were closed; the influential Lord's Day Observance Society could only suggest 'brighter worship'. For their part even some loyal citizens who were committed to the war effort came to 'resent the tremendous influx'. The impact of the military invasion was aggravated by the arrival of others from Britain — those transferred on government business and, by December 1940, some 1,600 evacuees. Many of these were schoolchildren, expectant mothers etc., who had come over in increasing numbers after the intensive raids on Coventry, Birmingham and Liverpool. In addition, there were those who had settled unofficially. The overall result was that available accommodation throughout much of the north was stretched to the limit, and rents were inflated, whilst road surfaces were pulverised by the unusual volume of heavy vehicles. Above all, even Woodside was concerned that the British forces in particular were 'eating up all the food'. By late 1941, as the threat of invasion receded, she records a growing local perception that they should be dispatched to help Russia or at least be given 'something to do'.[11]

Anthony Eden, Secretary of State for War, during a two-day tour of inspection of B.T.N.I. training centres near the border
Belfast Telegraph

Limits to the Disruptive Impact of War

Nonetheless, despite accumulating wartime disruption, Mrs Woodside was fully justified in describing Northern Ireland, in March 1940, as 'probably the pleasantest place in Europe'. She explained 'we are unbombed, we have no conscription, there is still plenty to eat and life is reasonably normal'.[12] Though food in the north had become scarcer, it was still more readily available than in Britain — milk remained plentiful throughout the war, vegetables and unrationed cuts of pork were generally obtainable and, until mid-1941, eggs were in ample supply. In Fermanagh, local people noticed young English soldiers sending food parcels home to their families. One Royal Navy sailor in Londonderry described it as 'a land flowing with milk and honey for us, where such unheard-of luxuries as steaks could be had in restaurants, and butter in lumps instead of thin slithers'.[13] Douglas Harkness, a leading Stormont civil servant, in the Ministry of Agriculture, likewise recorded after visiting Whitehall 'I was thankful to get back to Northern Ireland and the relative peace and plenitude that prevailed there'; in London it was 'queues and queues and nothing'.[14] The province was a major food-exporting region, and farmers responded well to calls for increased production, though their output was more scrupulously monitored by the authorities and transported to Britain in increasing volumes as the war

North Irish Horse, Rolls Royce armoured car crossing a bridge over the River Bush, Co Antrim
Public Record Office of Northern Ireland

progressed. Golf courses were used for grazing, and allotments proliferated. Even the lawns at Queen's University, Belfast were 'ploughed up for victory' and allocated to staff without gardens of their own.

Those living in border areas could most easily cross to the south to do their shopping; grocery stores even in small villages in Eire had a range of goods which northerners, by 1941, found breathtaking — butter, eggs, meat, cheese, bacon, jam, chocolate, cigarettes and lighters. Smuggling was rife, as it had been even before the war, and southern customs officials generally not overly officious. Along the Monaghan border, cattle were a significant element in the illegal cross-border trade. In Fermanagh, Breege McCusker recalls: 'one train that went to Bundoran became known as the sugar train as it had so many smugglers on board. Many a skinny female went down on the morning train to return on the evening one heavily pregnant'.[15] The Friday night service from Londonderry to St Johnston in Co. Donegal fulfilled a similar function: garda reported that smuggling was on a 'very large scale' locally.[16] Conscious that children were used in this clandestine trade, the Roman Catholic Bishop of Derry, Neil Farren, spoke out strongly in 1942, asking '...what hope can we have for the future... if even at an impressionable age they are trained in lying and deceit?'[17]

Professor T.T. Flynn, with his wife. He was Belfast's Chief Casualty Officer, and father of Errol
Public Record Office of Northern Ireland

On Carlingford Lough, the local police were aware that a 'system of barter'[18] had developed between smugglers on either side. Both oil-powered and rowing boats were used to transport flour, tea, rice and paraffin oil to Eire in exchange for sugar, eggs, butter and clothing. As elsewhere along the border, volumes are impossible to quantify but local garda reports give some impression of the scale of activity in the area. They carried out 183 petty seizures of smuggled goods in Omeath, Co. Louth, alone in June-July 1941; they estimated that 100 tons of flour had recently arrived in the south. In response to the extent of the illicit trade, the British government issued a regulation to the effect that rowing boats could not be used in United Kingdom tidal waters without a permit from the naval authorities.[19]

Overall, an RUC dispatch concluded that a 'condition of affairs arose [along the border] that shattered all pre-conceived ideas of smuggling'. The

Inspector-General, Charles Wickham, reported that 'ordinary consumers, speculators and syndicates commenced to export all classes of goods, including foodstuffs, to Eire and there was a danger that Northern Ireland would be denuded of much-needed supplies which in turn would have a damaging effect on the war effort'.[20] British civil servants described it as a 'lucrative, congenial and successful trade',[21] so much so that inevitably court cases arose in which it was alleged that customs officials and police officers were 'acting in collusion' with the smugglers.[22] After 12 tea chests had been seized on the southern side of the border near Keady, Co. Armagh, the garda superintendent for the division asserted in his report of 12 May 1941...'It is common knowledge that smugglers can arrange to have a clear road along border areas in Northern Ireland for their illegal traffic at times arranged for them by some of the police force there'. In the local idiom, the road was 'paid for'.[23] As a means of containing the temptation to become involved, payments to the RUC for successful operations against smugglers were increased. By December 1944, garda believed that the financial rewards being paid to members of the northern force were 'so good'[24] that it was encouraging them to cross the border in hot pursuit of suspects. As a result of such incentive schemes, various legislative initiatives and regulations, and occasional gun battles between security forces and smugglers, the extent of the illicit smuggling was reduced to more acceptable levels. The practice nonetheless helped fuel an active black market. Consequently by 1941 some had come to welcome the extension of rationing as a means of ensuring a more equitable distribution and reducing queues. When it had first been introduced Sir Basil Brooke, the local Minister of Agriculture, recalled the existence of a 'body of opinion at Stormont ... which was ... outraged at the idea' because of the north's substantial food surplus.[25]

The strains of war were also eased for many living in Northern Ireland by weekends and holidays spent in Eire. Thousands travelled south regularly each year, including army personnel, civil servants and in particular a broad spectrum of the northern middle class. It provided a convenient escape from the deprivations of rationing, the inconvenience of the blackout, the profusion of military uniforms and the heavily censored, war-obsessed media. Douglas Harkness 'welcomed the opportunity to enjoy the flesh pots' across the border. He recorded during one visit 'all the talk was of the Spanish civil war ... the current war was never mentioned'.[26] He was also aware of considerable numbers of army officers newly arrived at Dun Laoghaire from Holyhead, wearing half uniforms, the usual concession when travelling in a neutral country.

Mrs Woodside described the south as 'almost the last corner in all Europe where the lights are still lit ... nowhere else ... would it be ... possible so completely to escape the war'. She recorded vividly the mass invasion of Donegal hotels by Belfast's wealthier citizens in August 1941, just shortly after the blitz. They played golf and bridge and enjoyed meals at tables 'groaning with food ... unbelievably plentiful ... at luxury level'. Dinner was a six-course meal, evening wear was obligatory, mink and silver fox furs were much in evidence and jewellery worn by wives in what appeared like competitive display. Amidst the indulgence and frivolity, wireless news transmissions were ignored; in previous years they had been listened to in hushed silence. Throughout the war Dublin likewise seemed to her 'as brilliant as ever'. The streets at night were as bright as daylight, she noted, 'with huge streetlights', shop windows ablaze and neon signs flashing; 'you could actually see what people were wearing'. Cars sped along its busy roadways and there was scarcely a uniform in sight. As the war progressed she noticed changes — the street lights were cowled, three shelters appeared in O'Connell Street, each reassuringly padlocked, and shortages did arise of

Combined Services (WHITE)	TEAMS	Irish Eleven (RED)
SIDLOW (I.T. Centre) Wolves & I.T.C.	Goal	KELLY (Belfast Celtic)
(10) BANKS (The Loyals) Bolton & Glentoran	Right Back	McMILLAN (Belfast Celtic)
(9) McINNES (The King's) Liverpool & Distillery	Left Back	McKEOWN (Cliftonville)
(8) TAYLOR (The King's) Liverpool & Distillery	Right Half	McMILLEN (Linfield)
(7) EASTDALE (Capt.) (The King's) Liverpool & Linfield	Centre Half	VERNON (Belfast Celtic)
(6) SMYTH (R.A.M.C.) Aberdeen & Glentoran	Left Half	McDERMOTT (Glentoran)
(5) BEST (Royal Navy) R.N. & Cliftonville	Outside Right	COCHRANE (Linfield)
(4) EASTHAM (The King's) Liverpool & Distillery	Inside Right	McALINDEN (Capt.) (Belfast Celtic)
(3) NEARY (P.T.C.) Fulham & Glentoran	Centre Forward	D. WALSH (Linfield)
(2) DRURY (R.A.F.; Arsenal & Distillery	Inside Left	O'NEILL (Belfast Celtic)
(1) PATTERSON (The King's) Liverpool & Linfield	Outside Left	FEENEY (Derry City)

Referee—Mr. F. HUNTER
Linesmen—Messrs. E. SIMPSON and J. SLOAN

Red Cross nurses on parade at Mays' Market, Belfast
Ulster Museum

petrol, butter, tea, white flour, candles. Nonetheless this did nothing to dampen her enthusiasm or sense of release during visits to the 'capital city'.[27]

Culturally , Dublin had of course always been a more vibrant city than Belfast; in fact much of the latter's social life, like that of the north generally, survived the outbreak of hostilities more or less intact. One 150-year old tradition was broken — the normal twelfth of July demonstrations were suspended and replaced by religious services for the duration of the conflict. Cynics suggested that this was done to divert attention from the large number of able-bodied Orangemen who had not entered military service. In Northern Ireland church bells continued to ring; in Britain they were banned, except to announce invasion. Sporting venues, theatres and dance halls remained open throughout the war, their adverts filling the columns of local newspapers. Association football suffered less than elsewhere in the United Kingdom. No limits were imposed on crowd attendances at matches. Without conscription, there was no need to cancel players' contracts. Public interest was sustained through the availability of top quality guest players from locally-based military units, and the running of regional, and even national competitions. Cinemas also prospered — they offered warmth and entertainment and, unlike Britain, their doors stayed open during the autumn of 1939. In the late '30s, Belfast had 35 cinemas, with 28,000 seats, almost as many per head of population as London. Their seating capacity was stretched to the limit throughout most of the conflict. Apart from the contents of newsreels, and the presence of large numbers of servicemen (who numbered possibly one in six of Belfast cinema audiences by mid-1940) and of British evacuees, there was little to suggest that there was a war on. In 1943, the city's corporation agreed by a small majority to open them on Sundays — similar resolutions had been defeated in 1940 and 1942 — but access was permitted only to uniformed members of the armed forces.

Unemployment persists

The perpetuation of normality extended to other less desirable peacetime characteristics of life in Northern Ireland. The wartime contrast between important aspects of local experience and that found in Great Britain was pervasive and struck informed English visitors most forcefully. Harold Wilson (later prime minister, then a civil servant, he was secretary to the Imperial Manpower Requirements Committee of the war cabinet) arrived in Belfast during December 1940 to investigate the use being made of the province's manpower in war production. He was shocked to discover that 'after 15 months of war, far from becoming an important centre of munitions ... [it] ... had become a depressed area' both in relative and absolute terms and

Residents of Argyle Terrace,
Londonderry, trying on
their gas-masks
*Public Record Office of
Northern Ireland*

that its capacity was being grossly under-utilised. Not a single new factory had yet been constructed. The shipyards in Belfast alone had benefited from substantial government contracts; the first was received in September 1939, for 20 corvettes, and between 1939-1940, its workforce had risen from 17,850 to 24,390. Orders with other firms had been on an exceedingly meagre scale, even though suitable labour was available, the region had so far been immune from aerial attack, its ports were uncongested and its transport network relatively unstrained. At a time when British unemployment had halved, it had risen locally from 64,622 to 71,633, between September 1939 and November 1940 — a level similar to that found in the United Kingdom in 1932, the trough of the great depression. This was despite some voluntary recruitment and labour migration to Britain. Moreover, there was evidence that a number were not registering as unemployed, for fear of being compelled to join crown forces, or being sent to work in England, or because they had exhausted their claim to benefit. Wilson concluded that the result was widespread 'disappointment and disillusionment' within the Ulster workforce;[28] others claimed to detect a consequential increase in juvenile delinquency and also in political extremism.

The unionist leadership was convinced that if the number without work reached 100,000, it 'would have terrific repercussions on the government'.[29] It certainly damaged the province's image on the mainland. Midway through the war, a British newspaper described the 25,000 'young fit men and women' then in Ulster's dole queues as a 'disgrace to Britain and the Empire'.[30]

When Churchill was informed of the north's apparently negligible contribution to the war effort, he ordered an immediate investigation and instructed that requisite action should be taken to ensure that fuller use was made of its resources. It was, however, easier to describe and quantify Ulster's persistent unemployment problem than to resolve it. Its causes included the absence of conscription and the collapse of the local linen sector due to restrictions on raw material imports. The lack of munitions contracts for northern firms was partly because many lacked sufficient skilled labour and productive capacity, and their use raised transport problems not encountered in Britain. In addition, Belfast-based companies derived their electricity supply from the vulnerable corporation-run plant located inside the harbour estate. Imperial supply departments therefore preferred to rely on large established mainland firms, whilst they were still capable of expanding their output.

No Sense of War Urgency

Other aspects of life in the six counties which are less easily quantified also diverged starkly from British experience. This was immediately obvious to

A summer's day (June 1940) at the City Hall, Belfast
Ulster Folk and Transport Museum

Tom Harrisson, a professional wartime observer and founder of the Mass Observation Organisation. He arrived in June 1942, having just completed extensive studies of Merseyside and the Humber area. He had been analysing morale throughout Britain since the outbreak of war. He commented 'the lack of war urgency ... is most striking ... The atmosphere in Ulster is entirely different ... Many of the things which are taken for granted by the average Englishman or Scotsman ... like clothes rationing or transport difficulties ... are ... still the source of considerable irritation and resentment'. He described as 'typical' the response of a waitress in a restaurant when asked for sugar. She said loudly 'getting the sugar, getting the sugar, all day long I'm going from table to table getting this ruddy rationed sugar. I'm sick to death of the whole damn business. When will the war end and finish this rationing? Oh God, I wish that it would end and I wouldn't have to go round for the sugar.' Harrisson added that 'even the blitz on Belfast has not really awakened the people and it is regarded in some ways almost as an insult and a grievance'. He was conscious of the overall 'slackness in the atmosphere': it was so 'unmistakable' that he found himself 'constantly experiencing a curious sense of guilt at being there at all. It seemed somehow as if one was getting out of the war and having too easy a life.' He noted that 'people thought nothing of asking me to lunch and talking the whole afternoon. Being half an hour late for an appointment did not matter in the slightest, and perhaps the most curious shock of all is seeing men lying about in the morning on the grass outside the City Hall [Belfast] or sleeping with their feet up in the backs of cars. One realises that ... in Britain the whole tempo has changed from peacetime and anyone who behaved in a peacetime way now in London or Liverpool would at once be noticeable and might even cause a riot'.[31]

No conscription

There is no lack of evidence to corroborate these observations. An embarrassing symptom of local apathy from the viewpoint of the unionist cabinet was the relatively low recruitment level of volunteers for military service. In April 1939, Craig had urged that conscription be applied to Northern Ireland. The proposal immediately raised a storm of protest. Cardinal Joseph MacRory declared that it 'would be the greatest tyranny'[32] and that resistance was morally justified. De Valera said that, if imposed, it would equate to an 'act of war against our nation'.[33] Some Belfast trade union leaders and various Irish-American groups were also amongst those to voice their disapproval. The British press likewise broadly opposed its extension, fearing a recurrence of the unrest caused by the issue in Ireland during 1917-18. This hostile response was even referred to in a speech by Hitler, an expert on national minorities.

The province's 'special difficulties' were the reason given by Chamberlain to justify his government's decision not to introduce conscription. Lady Craigavon recorded in her diary

> the British government was frightened of the issue being complicated by Mr de Valera kicking up the dust, though Ulster affairs have nothing to do with him ... J. was asked flat out by Chamberlain 'is Ulster out to help in her war effort?' to which of course he answered 'you know we are'... Chamberlain then said 'if you really want to help us, don't press for conscription. It will only be an embarrassment'. What else could J. do than say 'Very well, I won't'.[34]

This outcome was denounced by Unionist MPs at Westminster. Basil Brooke expressed the bitterness felt within sections of the party and their perception of its cause. He reflected on their mood of 'resentment, anger and hurt pride at the feeling of having been snubbed'. He attributed the decision to the presence 'in their midst ... [of] ... a minority who whilst

22nd Battery of the 8th Belfast (Heavy Anti-Aircraft) regiment, Royal Artillery Supplementary Reserve, at Dunmore Camp on the eve of war, 1939
David Ashe, Langford Lodge Wartime Centre

prepared to share in the benefits of Empire ... were either afraid or too despicable to take a hand in the defence of the country who defended them and were prepared to go to any length to prevent the loyal and brave men ... from doing their duty'.[35]

During the opening phase of the war the 'loyal and brave' appeared to be numerous; recruits then came forward at a rate of 2,500 per month but, by the spring of 1940, the level had fallen to less than 1,000. This had prompted at least one attempt at private enterprise. At Queen's, the Vice-Chancellor, David Lindsay Kier, caused some resentment when he sent staff and students a circular letter stating that those who were physically fit had no reason to be attending university, and should enlist. A total of 2,335 university personnel joined the forces during the conflict, of whom 155 lost their lives. Kier himself was later knighted for his wartime services. Campbell College, Belfast, had probably the best recruitment record of any local educational institution — over 1,000 of its former pupils volunteered and 102 of these were killed in action.[36]

Concerned by the overall response, Craig persuaded a reluctant war office to sanction a local recruitment drive in May 1940. On his instruction it was aimed primarily at young men living in country districts; he also urged the necessity for tactful presentation to lessen the risk of civil disorder. A series of 20 rallies was held throughout Northern Ireland — the first at Belfast's Ulster Hall on 15 July 1940 and the last in Cookstown, Co Tyrone, seven weeks later. It had little measurable impact. The powerful folk memory of the carnage at the Somme in 1916 may have acted as a deterrent. The fluctuating monthly returns throughout the war were conditioned by a multitude of factors; these included the military situation itself, seasonal unemployment levels, the growing absorption of labour in war work and the variable needs of the services. Any upsurge in 1940 was short-lived and mainly occasioned by the brief wave of patriotic sentiment resulting from the evacuation of 300,000 allied troops from Dunkirk. Craig's choice of Sir Basil Brooke, the Minister of Agriculture, to spearhead the campaign is likely to have lessened the response from the catholic population; his reputation had been tarnished by a series of speeches he had made during 1933-34 encouraging Unionists to 'employ protestant lads and lassies'.[37] Also, he insensitively decided to use the Unionist Party machine for publicity purposes throughout. The frequent use of Lord Londonderry as a platform speaker may also seem inappropriate, given his pre-war contact with and apparent sympathy for the Nazi leadership. But Sir Basil had been impressed since by his commitment to allied victory, describing him as 'obsessed by the war. ... He ... talks of nothing else and feels that all that should be done is not being done.'[38]

The failure forced Craig to evaluate alternative measures to boost enlistment. For a time he considered the withholding of unemployment benefit from those men of military age who had failed to volunteer. This option was finally rejected after warnings from colleagues that the party would not 'stand behind us'.[39] Nonetheless Moya Woodside, who was actively involved in the administration of social services, noted in October 1940 that outdoor relief was 'being refused to single men here ... and the reason, although obvious, is not stated.'[40] By December 1940, monthly recruitment levels had fallen to roughly 600, and despite short-term variations the long-term trend was downward.

The Difficulties In The Munitions Industries

An equally disturbing symptom of the lack of 'war urgency' in Northern Ireland is provided by the performance of its major munitions industries. Certainly during the early stages of the conflict, they had collectively the worst production record of any region in the United Kingdom. When Brooke was appointed Minister of Commerce in late 1940, he found levels of output and productivity generally unsatisfactory, prolonged delays frequent in the completion of contracts, and hostile relations between management and labour in some leading local firms. (RUC records indicate that as many as 6,000 workers were prosecuted in the six counties for instigating strikes during the course of the war). When he sought orders from British supply departments, he was advised that he must first rectify these deficiencies. Ernest Bevin, Minister of Labour and National Service, predicted that Ulster would become 'a derelict province' after the war due to the combination of 'bad management' and 'workers slacking'.[41] He claimed, for example, that if Harland and Wolff was efficiently organised, its production could be raised by the equivalent of adding a further 7-8,000 men to admiralty shipyard labour in England. Even in 1943, its absenteeism levels were still twice that of the worst British yards. Brooke found the company uncooperative in its attitude towards his ministry, uninterested in the welfare of its workforce and unwilling to subcontract to neighbouring engineering works. He became convinced that the root cause was its incompetent leadership; its manager Sir Frederick Rebbick was criticised by officials for concentrating too much on post-war planning and reconstruction, at the expense of production to meet the immediate needs of the war. But other factors also help explain the firm's poor performance. These include the physical and psychological disruption caused by the blitz in 1941, and the fact that its output was comprised of a large proportion of difficult vessels and that it did extensive ship repair work, both of which dragged down productivity figures.

The Central Recruiting Office, Clifton Street, Belfast
Belfast Telegraph

Short and Harland had incomparably the worst strike record of any of the local munitions producers, whether gauged by the frequency of disputes, their duration, or the number of workers involved. Sir Wilfrid Spender, head of the Northern Ireland civil service, observed in 1940 that the company was a 'great disappointment'and was 'giving us a bad name across the water'.[42] Its morale was low and discipline poor; in late 1942 a well informed British official estimated that it was not working at more than 65% efficiency and that 'any amount of people [were] drawing pay for loafing about'.[43] On 13 April 1943, Lord Geddes informed the House of Lords that each aircraft which it constructed required 120,000 man-hours to complete, compared with an average of 40,000 for mainland firms. He laid the blame without equivocation on its directors. Civil servants at Stormont believed that its problems stemmed in part from the fact that it was such a young, inexperienced firm and had undergone a rapid growth in its labour force, which was drawn from 'all and sundry'.[44]

From September 1942, John Jestyn Llewellin, the British minister responsible for aircraft production, favoured placing the James Mackie and Sons foundry in charge of all aircraft production in Northern Ireland. At the time it was manufacturing munitions and also Sterling and Sunderland aircraft components. At Westminster, its wartime performance was considered to be exemplary — it was solicitous of the needs of its workforce, almost strike-free, and had made extensive use of available female labour. Nonetheless the proposal was ultimately rejected because of concern that it would in the short term at least disrupt local output levels and aggravate further labour relations at Shorts. Moreover, Stormont ministers shrank from the political consequences of such a decision.

Public Apathy Regarding Civil Defence

Public attitudes towards air raid precautions provide a further illustration of the contrast in atmosphere between Northern Ireland and Great Britain. Until April 1941, when Belfast experienced its first blitz, civil defence was widely regarded with indifference, even hostility, and it was difficult to raise sufficient recruits for the various services. There was a widespread conviction, initially shared by the government, that the province would not be attacked. It was assumed to be too remote and unimportant and in any case indirectly protected by Britain's defences, as Luftwaffe bombers based in northern Germany would have to cross over the British mainland to reach local targets. Days after war was declared, Lady Londonderry wrote to her husband 'all sorts of rot are going on here. Air raid wardens and blackouts! As if anyone cared or wished to bomb Belfast'.[45] As the prolonged immunity from attack continued, it encouraged speculation that de Valera had reached an understanding with Hitler that Irish neutrality would be respected both north and south of the border.

However, Government apprehension about the likelihood of a raid grew, especially after the Coventry attack on 14 November 1940, but by then it was too late either to provide adequate active or passive defences for the province or to dispel the deep-seated apathy of the civilian population. The rising tide of instructions and orders issued by Stormont continued to be regarded by the public as meddling and interference. Air raid wardens were perceived as objects of contempt and ridicule. In Moya Woodside's opinion they were 'young whippersnappers in uniform who enjoy displaying their authority'.[46] Jimmy Doherty, who joined the service early in the war, recalled how its members became 'a Keystone cop type of character ... the targets of comedians and cartoonists.' He experienced most initial opposition when attempting to take a census in working-class areas. The locals were suspicious of anyone asking personal questions; this response was 'a hangover from depression years',[47] as such activities were associated with visiting investigators enforcing hated means test regulations.

Blackout restrictions were poorly implemented. They were widely regarded as pointless, since Belfast would be easy for any aircraft to locate, especially as three quarters of Ireland was still lit up at night. In any case it soon became apparent they had not been effective in frustrating air raids in Britain. In early 1941, weeks before the blitz, blackout offences in Belfast had reached almost 1,000 per month and were beyond the capacity of its courts and

A barrage balloon in the grounds of R.B.A.I.; in the background, the Ritz
Public Record Office of Northern Ireland

magistrates to process. The government considered this response to be much worse than in any comparable urban area elsewhere in the United Kingdom. Similarly, gas masks were rarely carried — those doing so were assumed to be from Britain. When the first Luftwaffe attack on Belfast occurred, under one-sixth of its business premises had fire watchers on duty and a mere 4,000 women and children had been evacuated from the city. Successive official evacuation schemes had proved to be a fiasco, notwithstanding the German conquest of Holland, Belgium and northern France between 10 May and 22 June 1940. When the ministry organised the second movement on 29 August a mere 1,800 presented themselves at the boarding points; only 5,000 had registered their intention to participate in the first place.

At Christmas of that year a friend recently arrived from London warned Moya Woodside 'you are living in a fool's paradise over here.' She replied 'that may be [because] ... the precautions are half-hearted.' But she added 'we feel that we are another 240 miles there and back from Liverpool and why should the Germans bother coming all that distance'.[48] Early in 1941 a senior civil servant at Stormont reflected on the prevailing local 'disbelief ... in the possibility of raids.' He predicted 'a large number will dream until the bombs awake them'.[49] As a result, the impact of the raids was all the more traumatic. On 17 April 1941, a day after the first major assault on Belfast, a southern observer noted 'the people of Belfast were generally quite apathetic and did not appear to appreciate the vital necessity for air raid precautions. When a heavy air raid did occur they appear to have reacted in a manner which proves the great danger of false optimism.' He proceeded to describe 'panic-stricken' civilians fleeing from their homes into the open streets in affected areas as soon as the blitz began.[50]

2
LULL BEFORE THE STORM

Causes of the War's Limited Impact

The obvious contrast in outlook and behaviour which emerged between Northern Ireland and the rest of the United Kingdom is more easily described than accounted for. Tom Harrisson suggested that it was partly due to the 'cut-offness of Ulster' — its remoteness from the theatre of war and from Westminster. He wrote 'communication was so much delayed; censorship difficulties very much felt and resented. The free exchange of culture and personalities between Ulster and Britain, necessarily stopped by the war, has had astonishingly wide effects, working through the more intelligent people downwards'. He concluded, no doubt with justification, that this 'cut-offness is a serious obstacle to maximum war effort' in the province.[1]

Some government ministers, John McDermott in particular, acknowledged openly and with regret that Northern Ireland was 'only half in the war'.[2] He became convinced that the absence of conscription was a key determinant of local attitudes. Harrisson shared this view. He observed that 'nearly all the regulations applying in England, apply in Ulster with one exception ... it is the absence of conscription which very largely effects Ulster apathy'. He believed that by studying the Ulster situation 'one is able to see the enormous part which conscription has played in influencing Britain's psychology', both by 'increasing war awareness' and heightening 'psychological and social frictions and anxieties'. He related it closely to one other factor; 'everything in Ulster is intimately mixed with the religious dichotomy which divides the country into Catholics (mainly Nationalists) and Protestants (mainly Unionists)'. He stated that this deep sectarian division was the key factor in influencing Westminster's decision not to introduce conscription and implied that this characteristic was unique in the United Kingdom.[3]

The Quality of Political Leadership

Harrisson stressed, however, that the absence of a sense of war urgency was not only shared by both religious traditions but was a characteristic of all social levels, 'from the cabinet minister to remote peasant dwellings and the most distant points of the Antrim coast'.[4] Without doubt, much of the pervasive apathy was due to the inertia and laxity which shrouded most Stormont departments during the war-time premiership of James Craig and his successor John Andrews. Craig was a genial, unflappable Ulsterman of independent means who had entered politics in 1906 after military service in the Boer war. More than any other individual, he was responsible for the formation of Northern Ireland and it was therefore appropriate that he should become its first Prime Minister. However, more than anyone else, he was also to blame for its ultimate political collapse. Exhausted already by the demands of the pre-partition period and suffering thereafter from deteriorating health he failed entirely to devise any long-term strategy for the province

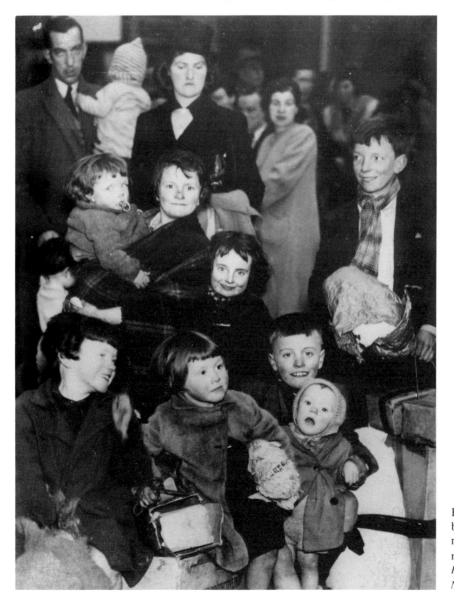

Belfast evacuees waiting to board; the social classes meet but do not necessarily mingle
Public Record Office of Northern Ireland

after 1922. His response to its deep sectarian divisions was to let matters drift rather than devise and implement policies directed towards its ultimate stability and survival.

Sir Wilfrid Spender, head of the local civil service, enclosed a memorandum in his private diary dated 2 August 1938. It was an insider's view of contemporary Northern Ireland politics and amounted to a devastating indictment of the collective incompetence of Craig and his cabinet colleagues. He itemised their grave policy 'mistakes' and misjudgements and expressed deep concern at the resulting decline in popular support and respect for their leadership. He reflected on the Prime Minister's alarming tendency to make important decisions in a casual, hasty manner and noted with apprehension that owing to the continuing deterioration in his health, he was then unable to perform more than one hour's work daily. He was convinced that Sir James was too unwell to carry on, though informed medical opinion warned that any drastic or enforced change in his lifestyle might prove fatal. Sir Wilfrid also considered that at least two other senior ministers ought to retire immediately on the grounds that they too were suffering from prolonged and incapacitating illness. He observed of a third that, although he was the main focus of public criticism of the government, he was nonetheless holidaying abroad at the time, adding that 'his decisions his officials can not count on'. He noted that as a consequence of the cabinet's shared inadequacy, the main burden of administration had come to rest on the willing, but ageing, shoulders of the Minister of Finance, J.M.Andrews (the average age of cabinet ministers in 1938 was 62 years.) Spender concluded dejectedly that if the present 'loose' conduct of affairs continued, it would do irreparable harm to the unionist cause and might even pose a threat to the survival of democracy itself in Northern Ireland.[5]

When war began 12 months later, the composition of the Stormont cabinet was unchanged. Against his own inclination, Craig had been persuaded by his wife to remain in office, mainly for reasons of financial necessity and social ambition; she was clearly unaware of the extent to which the progressive deterioration in his health had impaired his capacity for leadership. Until his death on 24 November 1940, he led his colleagues in increasingly dictatorial and whimsical fashion, in the process straining the proper functioning of the cabinet system almost to breaking point. He habitually reached important decisions without prior discussion with the appropriate ministers and on occasion encouraged individuals to act on their own responsibility or after consultation with himself. He brought his Chief Whip, Lord Glentoran, into his confidence more than the members of his government. Robert Gransden, the newly appointed Cabinet Secretary, also served as Sir James' private secretary. He resented as much as had his predecessor, Sir Charles Blackmore, running errands for the Craig household

— buying cigarettes or ordering marmalade from Fortnum and Mason's in London.

In 1940, the Stormont leadership was having to adopt some unusual tactics for controlling parliament. When, for instance, the Prime Minister's excessive salary and allowances came before the house for review (according to Spender, his income was greater than that of the British Prime Minister), the Chief Whip sought to reduce the time available for debate by providing unionist backbenchers with points on other matters with which they might criticise the government's record. He also arranged for Independent Labour MP, Jack Beattie, a voluble but not ineffective opposition member, to be detained in the commons bar. Apart from these desperate short-term stratagems, Craig's most characteristic response to the increasing gravity and volume of attacks on his administration was either to make grossly extravagant claims regarding the success of its policies, or to attempt to silence critics through concessions justified mainly by political expediency. These included dispensing grants and subsidies, and setting up parliamentary committees of enquiry (these could quite effectively silence opponents, as members were generously remunerated). His most important and valuable response was the creation of a new department, the Ministry of Public Security; its functions included 'public security, civil defence, the preservation of the peace and maintenance of order, the co-ordination of civil defence services and the protection of persons and property from injury or damage in the present emergency'.[6] J.C. MacDermott was appointed minister on 25 June 1940. He was a lawyer and King's Counsel and was at the time serving as an officer with the royal artillery, having enlisted in August 1939. He was, in addition, Unionist MP for Queen's University — one of the few constituencies prepared to select candidates such as himself who were not members of the Orange Order. His promotion owed much to the fact that his father knew Craig well.

The Prime Minister's initiatives, however, fell short of what his critics increasingly demanded — a change in the composition of the cabinet itself; between 1921-39 only twelve individuals served as members. Edmund Warnock, a junior minister, resigned over this issue on 25 May 1940. He accused his former colleagues of being slack, dilatory and apathetic and protested with justification that 'death, illness or promotion' were the only causes of cabinet change. He alleged that no-one had ever been replaced 'because of incompetence or failure'.[7] In mid-June a second junior minister, Lieutenant-General Robert Gordon, left the government for similar reasons; he unreservedly condemned its 'lack of drive and initiative and utter lack of what war means'.[8] Most contemporary criticism of the Stormont leadership focused on its persistent failure to reduce unemployment or to make adequate provision for civil defence and on its alleged equivocation over introducing

urgently needed reforms in such key areas as education, transport and electricity supply. The alarming deterioration in the strategic position of the western allies by June 1940, and the formation of a new and dynamic administration at Westminister during the previous month, made the fumbling ineptitude of Craig and his cabinet appear even more indefensible.

Spender was particularly concerned about the entirely unsatisfactory relationship between the Minister of Home Affairs, Dawson Bates, and the British military authorities based in Northern Ireland. Bates apparently refused to reply to army correspondence. As a result, General Sir Herbert J. Huddleston, who had served as GOC in the province, raised the question directly with George VI, who subsequently discussed it in person with the Northern Ireland premier. Considerations such as this caused Spender to predict that the imperial government would be compelled ultimately to impose martial law on Ulster, with the permanent secretaries of the Stormont departments taking over some of the functions previously exercised by local ministers. Earlier, in December 1939, he had ruefully observed 'there is one factory in which we could probably claim that we or the Free State are the largest manufacturers — namely the factory of grievances'.[9]

Agricultural Response To The Challenge Of War

From the government's perspective, Northern Ireland's 'best story' in this period was the dynamic performance of the region's farmers. During late 1939, the Ministry of Agriculture at Stormont became responsible for the purchase, distribution and sale of food produced locally and for stimulating increased output. Its greatest initial challenge arose from an agreement which it reached with Whitehall, that Ulster producers should increase their total area under tillage from the current 150,000 acres to 250,000, during 1939-40. To some MPs, it appeared to be an impossible task. But the sector had the incentive of large, stable markets and attractive guaranteed prices (for the first time identical locally to those offered in Britain). Moreover, agricultural machinery was made available at low cost. Failure by individuals to comply with departmental quotas could lead to the loss of their holding. Brooke, the minister responsible and the most energetic cabinet member, much preferred persuasion and, supported by civil servants of exceptional quality, launched a vigorous publicity campaign. They made appeals on the wireless, visited fairs and markets, and a personal letter was sent to each farmer, signed by Sir Basil. The results were impressive — Northern Ireland, alone of all the regions in the United Kingdom, exceeded its target in 1940. Its tillage acreage had by then reached 270,000; the expansion was sustained — by 1943 the figure was 850,000 acres. Despite criticisms of the ministry's allegedly dictatorial powers, profligate spending, and somewhat insensitive appeals for more Sunday working, this consistent record of achievement created a uniquely favourable impression at Stormont. Even in 1940, those travelling across the province marvelled at the 'fields and fields of hay, corn, flax, sheep, cattle, root crops'.[10]

John MacDermott as Minister of Public Security

This apart, the newly appointed Minister of Public Security, John MacDermott, showed energy and commitment in trying to increase Northern Ireland's preparedness for Luftwaffe attack. Probably from his first day in office, he was convinced that the province's immunity hitherto could not last indefinitely. He had been appalled to discover that, as late as 1940, fire-fighting equipment had been returned to Britain by the Home Affairs ministry, acting on the assumption that it would not be needed in the six counties. In the meantime, however, most ministers had come to acquire a keener sense of reality and proportion. Several factors heightened their awareness of Northern Ireland's vulnerability . The fall of France increased fears of a German invasion of Ireland. It also immediately accentuated the strategic significance of Britain's north-west ports; from late summer, those on the mainland were the objective of a major Luftwaffe offensive. The likelihood that this might be extended to Northern Ireland was increased in 1941, when more munitions contracts began to be awarded to local firms as mainland industry approached maximum output. From September 1940 onwards, enemy reconnaissance aircraft were reported over the province with increasing frequency. It has since become clear that they were preparing target files for a later assault on its major munitions producers, docks, airports and public utilities. It was in this context that a determined but sadly belated attempt was made to strengthen the province's active defences, especially around Belfast and Londonderry, and to accelerate recruitment to and improve the efficiency of the civil defence services. Apathy persisted at all levels, supplies of essential equipment were scarce and, above all, time was short. On 29

The Auxiliary Fire Service, Belfast, being inspected by J.C. MacDermott, then Minister of Public Security
Public Record Office of Northern Ireland

March 1941, MacDermott concluded a letter to Andrews with remarks which proved to be prophetic. He stated 'up to now we have escaped attack. So had Clydeside until recently. Clydeside got its blitz during the period of the last moon ... the period of the next moon, from say, the 7th to the 16th of April, may well bring our turn'.[11] At the time of writing Belfast was, in his opinion, less well defended than any comparable industrial city or port in Great Britain.

Arrest of Enemy Aliens; Internment of Republican Suspects

One feature of life in Northern Ireland surprised Tom Harrisson during his visit in 1942. Given the general atmosphere of apathy and lethargy, he stated 'one might expect security to be particularly lax ... on the contrary, it is superior to the English average'.[12] In this one sector, Stormont ministers displayed their customary zeal and the measures which they implemented compared favourably with any region in Britain. The steps taken locally were largely initiated by Westminster and were applicable throughout the United Kingdom. These included the introduction of an identity card system, restrictions on travel, the censorship of mail and of trunk calls, and controls on the press. As elsewhere, a register of enemy aliens was compiled in the autumn of 1939; it included 200 Germans, 32 Austrians, 24 Czechs and 155 Italians. Generally they had arrived in the province over the previous three years, fleeing from fascist persecution in central Europe; (many of their compatriots, applying for permission to settle, were refused entry, either to Northern or to southern Ireland). Most were arrested during the spring of 1940, and many interned at Huyton on the Isle of Man, a camp holding at the time roughly 3,000 captives. Walter Storch, a wealthy Austrian Jew, was typical. He had been held at Buchenwald concentration camp with his parents (who eventually died there) but successfully bribed his way to freedom. He settled first in Eire in 1938, and then moved north to Belfast before being interned two years later.

Moya Woodside was a member of a committee concerned with the welfare of enemy aliens and recorded their wartime experiences with great sympathy. In 1940, she noted 'we know from the police that there is not a single refugee out of 4-500 in Ulster who has not at one time or another been accused (without proof) ... of being a Nazi spy'. In her view, those who were interned suffered not only the injustice, deprivation and hardship of incarceration, but also considerable mental anguish through being separated from families only recently uprooted from their own homelands. They felt a strong sense of betrayal because, as one explained, 'the country which gave them protection from Nazi persecution and which now proclaims that it is fighting for liberty and justice, locks them up behind barbed wire and treats them worse than prisoners of war'. But, she claimed, 'their troubles only begin when they get out'; employers were reluctant to re-employ them (many were highly skilled or academically well-qualified), and due to the atmosphere of suspicion aroused by their detention, 'no-one wants to have aliens in the house'. As a result, a number suffered acute nervous anxiety and strain, and an observable physical deterioration. In early 1941, the Ulster coastline was 'suddenly and without warning' declared a protected area, and refugees living or working there were required to leave at a few days' notice.[13]

However, by no means all the actions taken by the authorities in the province were a mere replication of those being implemented in Great Britain. As Blake writes in his official war history, 'the British in their extremity could ... take no risks. [But] ... in Northern Ireland, the dangers ... were all the greater because of the open frontier with Eire, and the existence of a potential fifth column in the Irish Republican Army'.[14] Harrisson likewise attributed the 'superior' quality of security in the north to 'the constant fear of IRA activity going back for decades among the predominantly protestant police force, [which] leads to an alertness which is not essentially related to the war'.[15] Thus, on the first night of hostilities, an internment order was implemented (it had last been applied on a substantial scale in November 1938, when 'all the principal officers in the Belfast Battalion were caught and interned')[16] and 45 republican suspects were arrested. The government, acting on the advice of Charles Wickham, RUC Inspector-General, asked Westminster to establish a camp at Ballykinlar not only for accepting enemy aliens, but in the interests of the defence of the realm. In May 1940, a further 76 suspects were interned, with plans to arrest another 700. By 1942, the number detained had risen to 802, 450 of them held in Crumlin Road jail, Belfast, and the remainder on a prison ship, recently acquired from Britain anchored in Belfast Lough. The IRA's estimated strength was 2,000 in May 1941.

Amongst the most controversial measures taken was the internment in Brixton jail, on 11 July 1941, of Cahir Healy (Nationalist MP for the Westminister constituency of Fermanagh and Tyrone). He had been arrested in similar circumstances during the troubles of the early twenties. The RUC alleged that he had been involved in seditious activity, but that it was 'impossible to get witnesses to come forward in open court' to provide the necessary evidence.[17] The precise nature of any offence he may have committed is unclear; it has been suggested that he may have written to the German minister in Dublin or sent a letter to a catholic priest in Newtownbutler inquiring as to the prospects of Irish unity after a German invasion. Moya Woodside considered that his arrest was like 'kidnapping an innocent citizen'.[18] Similarly, Douglas Harkness, a civil servant who knew

Lord Gort, Inspector-
General of Training, on a
tour of inspection, February
1941, at Magilligan Point
*David Ashe, Langford Lodge
Wartime Centre*

Healy, regarded him as being 'as sound a conservative as I am ... I could not believe that the man I had known would have aided the enemy in any way'.[19] De Valera refused to intervene officially, replying to requests to do so made in the Dail that 'it would not achieve its object.'[20] The MP was eventually released in December 1942.

Meanwhile, from late 1939, special constabulary patrols were increased (the force's strength was then about 12,500), territorials and royal engineers guarded the coastal defences, and the movement of persons across the Irish border was closely monitored. Harrisson was particularly impressed by the security consciousness evident in the urban areas which he visited. At the quayside in Londonderry, he noted that ...'Naval sentries with fixed bayonets [stood] at the land end of each landing stage or pier.' In Belfast, he found that it was harder to enter the docks than anywhere else he had previously studied in Britain. Every possible access point was well guarded, usually by two or more policemen, armed with revolvers and rifles. In both cities, ships were carefully inspected and the RUC patrolled the port area, some in plain clothes.[21]

Building up of security forces

During the first 15 months of war, the security forces were strengthened by the addition of increasing numbers of British troops. Far from protecting the province from a surprise German attack, most of these were initially located entirely with a view to internal security. On 2 September 1939, General R.V. Pollock, who then commanded the British army's Northern Ireland District, held the opinion that 'if trouble comes to this country, it will come from within the borders'.[22] Toward the end of October, units of the 53rd (Welsh) Division began to arrive and were deployed at Lisburn, Belfast, Londonderry and Ballymena. According to the division's official history, neither enemy seaborne or air attack was anticipated and 'the chief reason' for their being transferred from Britain was 'the activities of the so-called IRA'. This continued to be the case until the early summer of 1940 and 'resulted in much dislocation of training'. With the fall of France, the main function of the troops was 'completely changed. What had almost entirely been an internal security problem became one of anti-invasion.'[23]

In mid-1940, public hysteria over the possibility that Britain itself would be invaded, and the consequential emergence of unregulated militias, resulted in a prompt political response. On 14 May, Sir Anthony Eden announced that recruiting had begun for a new force known as the Local Defence Volunteers (1.8 million men were eventually raised). Soon afterwards, the imperial government permitted Stormont to emulate these protection arrangements within Northern Ireland. On 28 May the scheme was announced, but it was not implemented on the same basis as elsewhere in the United Kingdom. Craig, of his own volition and despite strong opposition protests, decided that the B Specials should form its nucleus; he considered that a policy of open enrolment would merely facilitate republican infiltration. It was therefore raised as a branch of the special constabulary — whose sub-commandants selected 'suitable' candidates within their own locality. Morever, the force was placed under the authority of the RUC Inspector-General not, as in England, under military command. There was therefore obvious justification in Moya Woodside's observation that the government had succeeded in transforming it into a 'sectarian body'.[24] MacDermott recalled that a few Catholics did enlist, but that 'virtually all left because they hated the B Specials'.[25] In parliament, it was alleged that members of the minority community had been turned away. The Prime Minister also extravagantly, but characteristically, claimed in the Commons that the LDVs had been recruited, armed, and placed on duty within one week of his personal appeal for volunteers. This assertion was the immediate cause of A.R.G. Gordon's decision to resign as parliamentary and financial secretary at the Ministry of Finance. He regarded Sir James' statement as misleading, and the figures cited as being at complete variance with his own. Nonetheless, by August 1940, over 26,000 had enrolled . In 1941, on Churchill's insistence, the title LDV (nicknamed locally 'look, duck, and vanish brigade') was changed

Local Defence Volunteers (Home Guard) march through Belfast city centre on their way to training, 31 May, 1941
Belfast Telegraph

to Home Guard — by then it had a more adequate allocation of uniforms and weapons, and training manuals had been made available. It was trained in guerrilla tactics in case of invasion, manned anti-aircraft batteries in Belfast and Londonderry and was deployed in the defence of government buildings, munitions factories, public utilities and airfields, and in helping check documents of identity.

Meanwhile, the way in which the Ulster Home Guard had been raised had become a matter of growing controversy in Britain. Prominent Home Guard leaders in London signed a petition, directed at the Westminster government, calling for an end to the sectarianism of the force in Northern Ireland. Dr Bernard Griffin, the Roman Catholic Archbishop of Westminster, wrote a letter of support to Downing Street. Aware that the issue would have potential repercussions among catholic communities throughout the United Kingdom, Churchill requested the views of the Home Office, War Office and Dominions Office on whether the Home Guard should be transferred from police to military control within the six counties.[26] The Home Secretary, Herbert Morrison, favoured taking action on political grounds. He stated that 'there are Catholics...[there]...who would join the imperial defence forces but are unwilling to join a force administered by a government which they regard as a sectarian government'.[27] The War Office opposed intervening in the province's affairs. David Margesson, the Secretary of State, observed: 'I feel so strongly that on the grounds of both military efficiency and of the absolute necessity of not involving the army in the religious animosities of Ireland we should not offer to take over this force.'[28]

Churchill would have preferred to let sleeping dogs lie, but the Northern Ireland government rendered this option problematic. They asked that, if London chose not to act, they be given permission to announce that

> the imperial authorities, having considered the offer made by the government of Northern Ireland to transfer the Local Defence Volunteer section of the Ulster Constabulary to the control of the Army Council, had requested the government to maintain the force as a branch of the Ulster Special Constabulary.[29]

Ultimately, Sir John Anderson, the Lord President of the Council, was asked to assess the situation, and concluded that Catholics were unlikely to join a predominantly protestant force no matter who controlled it. Subsequently, in March 1941, it was decided to inform the Stormont cabinet, with the minimum possible publicity, that the *status quo* would remain undisturbed. John MacDermott announced on 27 March that 'His Majesty's government have come to the conclusion that it is the interests of administrative efficiency and convenience that the force be maintained as a branch of the constabulary force under the control of the government of Northern Ireland until such time as it may be necessary for the military authorities to assume control of the force for operational purposes'.[30]

In retrospect, these security measures may be regarded as justified and successful, given the relative absence of internal disorder during the war. When MI5 officers visited Northern Ireland in August 1940, Sir Charles Wickham reassured them that there was little chance of an IRA armed rising in the north (whether timed to coincide with a German invasion or otherwise). He 'pointed out that quite apart from the armed forces, there is now in ... [the six counties] ... a force of some 40,000 armed men, Protestants'[31] — the combined strength of the B Specials and the LDVs. In fact, despite this and the increasingly disruptive impact of internment, the IRA did sustain a limited measure of scattered and partially co-ordinated activity throughout the six counties for most of the war. During April and May 1940, there were 13 shops bombed in Belfast and country towns, and occasional raids on banks, police barracks and military camps. On 11 February 1940, a successful attack was carried out on a Royal Irish Fusiliers store at Ballykinlar, Co. Down. The peak year was 1942. It began with a robbery at the ARP office in Academy Street, Belfast, and continued with attacks on RUC personnel in Belfast, Dungannon, Strabane, Claudy, and the Crossmaglen area. It reached a climax with the arrest of Hugh McAteer, the Chief of Staff, and the imposition of a curfew on the Falls Road area of the city. Thereafter IRA activity dwindled.

This desired outcome was also due in part to the effective measures taken by the London and Dublin governments; both were concerned at the danger which the IRA posed. On 12 January 1939, the organisation (despite serious internal dissensions) had in effect declared war on England, sending an ultimatum to Lord Halifax, the Foreign Secretary, demanding Britain's withdrawal from the six counties within three days, and signed by Patrick Flemming. On 15 January, a publicly-displayed proclamation announced the outbreak of hostilities on behalf of the 'Republican government and the Army Council of Oglaigh na hEireann'.[32] The next day bombs exploded in London, Liverpool, Manchester, Birmingham and elsewhere. Over the following five months, the IRA was responsible for 127 incidents on the mainland, almost half of them in London, causing one death and 55 injuries. The Nazi newspaper, the *Volkischer Beobachter*, commented 'the Irish republicans are in earnest, for all their fantasy'.[33] Gradually the British government built up counter-measures in response, and these ultimately proved to be effective. By June 1939, a large quantity of bomb-making equipment had been recovered and 66 suspects arrested. These included a 16 year-old Dubliner, Brendan Behan, who was convicted for his alleged part in causing two huge explosions at Hammersmith Bridge, London, on 29 March. By 29 July, the Prevention of Violence Act had passed through Westminister; it gave the authorities new powers of detention and required all Irish nationals to register with the police, as other aliens were obliged to do. Within days 50 republican suspects were deported, whilst many others fled the country before orders could be served. A brief final flurry of violence followed. The worst incident was an explosion in Coventry, on 25 August. A bomb in a bicycle carrier-basket, discarded by a volunteer who had panicked before reaching his agreed target, exploded in the busy Broadgate shopping area. Five people were killed instantly and a further 69 injured. As a result 'Irish houses' in the city were searched, five individuals charged and on 7 February 1940, two of them — James McCormick and Peter Barnes — executed.[34]

While the British government was stepping up its security measures, so too did the authorities in Dublin. They were initially alarmed by the daring IRA raid on the magazine fort in Phoenix Park, Ireland's 'Fort Knox', on 23 December 1939, in which over one million rounds of ammunition were seized. Four weeks earlier, £5,000 had been stolen from a post office in Dublin's city centre and on 3 January 1940, a police officer was murdered in Patrick Street, Cork. Irish military intelligence was also aware that the IRA was in contact with the German *Abwehr*; it suspected that its contact with the Nazis dated back to when Sean MacBride had been active in the force (he was Chief of Staff 1936-7). Certainly Berlin sought, with the help of Irish republican collaborators, to prepare the ground for a peaceable invasion of the island. Dermot Keogh writes: 'with the help of the IRA most of the country would have been turned into a Gaelic Vichy had the Nazis taken control'.[35] In May 1940, Neville Chamberlain thought that the organisation was 'almost strong enough to overrun the weak Eire forces' and warned that an enemy landing might be imminent.[36]

In response, the Dublin government devised a general defence plan which assumed that any German invasion would be conducted in conjunction with an internal republican rising. Joseph Walshe considered that, if the Germans attacked, it would provide 'the opportunity they [ministers] were seeking...to crush finally' the IRA.[37] In any case, they took stern measures to deal with the perceived threat from within. By August 1942, six IRA members had been executed, all but one for murder (meanwhile by October 1942, six Garda officers had been murdered by the IRA). In addition, two IRA volunteers were shot dead by the Garda while resisting arrest and three others died on hunger strike. Also in the course of the war, over 1,000 detention orders were made for IRA members, 400 were sentenced to terms of imprisonment and roughly 1,100 were taken into custody — 600 was the largest number at any one time. The northern government considered that the emergency powers regarding internment in the south were more substantial and more rigorously applied than its own.[38]

1940; A Bargain? — Irish Unity For Neutrality

During the late spring of 1940, the vigorous security precautions being taken by the Northern Ireland government were overshadowed by events which seemed infinitely more grave and were certainly more divisive. From April onwards Stormont ministers and officials watched the Anglo-Irish trade talks, then being conducted in London, with growing apprehension. They feared that constitutional issues would be raised and possibly a deal struck, in which de Valera would offer, or be asked, to abandon Irish neutrality in exchange for the ending of partition. Sir Basil Brooke stated privately that this would be a 'very difficult nut to crack'.[39] The whole question raised a potentially critical clash of interests between the two United Kingdom governments as well as a deep conflict of loyalty within Northern Ireland itself.

Undoubtedly some British ministers and military advisers would have favoured some such understanding with the south — they were increasingly anxious to gain access to its airfields and the Treaty ports as the allies strategic position crumbled. On 10 May, Germany invaded the Low Countries; on 3 June the British evacuation from Dunkirk was completed, and one week later Italy entered the war. The sight of Nazi troops goose-stepping into Paris was described in the *Daily Mail* (15 June 1940) as 'the blackest scene in history'. On 22 June, France signed a humiliating armistice; Petain had already emerged as a collaborationist leader. In Churchill's phrase, Britain faced the 'abyss of a new dark age'.[40] Spender thought the 'European position to be so serious that there is no knowing what sacrifices [it would] be necessary for Northern Ireland to make'.[41]

Already on 1 June, acting on information from intelligence sources, the British government warned Dublin that an IRA-supported invasion was imminent and would precede an assault on England. On 12 June, Neville Chamberlain wrote to Churchill, Prime Minister since 10 May, urging that a conference be held between de Valera and Craig in London, to secure their cooperation in defence preparations. Over the next few weeks Craig came under more intense persuasion, cajolement and political pressure from Westminister than at any time since November 1921. Initially on 5 June, he was asked to make constructive suggestions as to how the Taoiseach might be drawn into meaningful discussions about the defence of the 32 counties, and one week later was summoned to attend more open-ended discussions with the southern leader. His response was as inflexible as it had been 20 years before. His priority remained the preservation of the six counties within the United Kingdom. He adamantly refused to participate in an inter-governmental conference before the south had abandoned its neutrality, and in any circumstances if constitutional matters were to be considered.

Surprisingly perhaps, this response was not supported unanimously by Craig's ministerial colleagues. During the heat of the crisis there were indications of a split emerging within the Stormont cabinet. Both Sir Basil Brooke and John MacDermott were prepared to accept changes in Northern Ireland's constitutional status, if in response Eire proved willing to enter the war on the allied side. In their view loyalty to king and empire and the defeat of the Axis powers transcended their commitment to the union. John Brooke later summarised his father's view: 'if we were faced with the choice of losing our civilisation or accepting the unification of Ireland ... he would have to do his best to secure Irish unity'.[42] In fact, though the crisis passed without the issue being put to the test, the anxiety felt at Stormont was fully justified.

When his proposed inter-governmental conference failed to materialise, Chamberlain was given approval by the war cabinet (16 June) to send Malcolm MacDonald (Minister for Health) to Dublin. His purpose was to discuss with de Valera issues arising from the prospect of a German attack. They met on three occasions, 17, 21 and 26 June, and a number of proposals were discussed, including the unification of Ireland. The British government was prepared to give 'a solemn undertaking that the union of Ireland would become an accomplished fact at an early date. There would be no turning back from that declaration'. It suggested that a joint body formed by the Belfast and Dublin governments could begin immediately to work out the practical details. In return Ireland was 'forth-with [to] enter into the war on the side of the United Kingdom and her allies'.[43]

In Belfast when Craig was informed of the terms being offered (on 26 June), he immediately dispatched a telegram to Chamberlain. It stated: 'Am profoundly shocked and disgusted by your letter making suggestions so farreaching behind my back and without any pre-consultation with me full stop to such treachery to loyal Ulster I will never be a party.'[44] In response Chamberlain expressed 'regret you should make such unfair charge against this government' and advised 'please remember the serious nature of the situation which requires that every effort be made to meet it'.[45] Craig, in reply, stated his 'conviction' that de Valera 'is under German dictation and far past reasoning with full stop he may purposely protract negotiations till enemy has landed full stop strongly advocate immediate naval occupation of harbours and military advance south'.[46]

Meanwhile in Dublin there is strong evidence of division within the Irish government on how best to respond to the British offer but in the end it was rejected. Even before the war, when de Valera was asked hypothetically would he abandon neutrality to achieve unity, he had reacted coolly; he had stated 'that is to ask shall we barter our right to freedom in order to secure our right to unity'.[47] When in June 1940 the hypothesis became reality, there were powerful arguments for rejection. MacDonald himself expected a negative reply; he wrote 'I feel that their attitude would be different if they had not an impression that we were going to lose.'[48] Joseph Walshe, Secretary of the Department of External Affairs in Dublin, was particularly pessimistic, stating his conviction that 'Britain's defeat has been placed beyond all doubt...England is already conquered'. (He derived some comfort from the belief that Hitler's 'real aim is the building up of a new Europe under German leadership';[49] as this would require US friendship, which Germany would jeopardise if it invaded Ireland, he regarded invasion as unlikely.) Moreover Ireland lay virtually undefended against either air or seaborne attack. During the early stages of the war its active defences were comprised of just eight aircraft, four search lights and four anti-aircraft guns. In May 1940, the Chief of Staff's considered view was that there was 'no striking force available capable of offering organised resistance to an enemy'.[50] There was in addition at the time a deep distrust of the British government as to whether it would or could deliver Irish unity. Dublin ministers were especially suspicious of Churchill; certainly he opposed 'the coercion of Ulster', but was 'much in favour of their being persuaded'.[51] In a reference back to the Great War, de Valera remarked 'I said our people had heard that tale once before ... We know what thanks we got [then]'.[52]

Later in the war some of these issues were reopened once again. During the discussions with MacDonald the southern government had assumed that the United States' policy of neutrality would continue indefinitely. After Pearl Harbour (7 December 1941) and American entry on the side of the allies, there was speculation that these events might cause a shift in Dublin's policy. At 4.00a.m. on 8 December, Churchill sent a telegram to de Valera stating 'Now is your chance. Now or never. "A nation once again"'.[53] At least one Irish minister formed the opinion ...'that Churchill had been imbibing heavily that night'.[54] The Taoiseach interpreted the message as an offer of unity (the British Prime Minister later denied this imputation, saying he 'certainly contemplated no deal on partition').[55] In a speech delivered in Cork, on 14 December 1941, he reiterated and sought to justify his government's policy towards the conflict. He declared 'we can only be a friendly neutral. ... From the moment ... the war began, there was for this state only one policy possible — neutrality. Our circumstances, our history, the incompleteness of our national freedom through the partition of our country, made any other policy impracticable. Any other policy would have divided our people'.[56] Lemass likewise thought that 'any departure from [neutrality] would provoke a disastrous civil war'.[57] De Valera wrote in similar vein in March 1944, stating that 'neutrality represents the united will of the people and parliament. It is the logical consequence of Irish history and of the forced partition of our national territory'.[58] When the Australian Prime Minister, Robert Menzies, heard of de Valera's position — Irish unity, combined with continued neutrality and the withdrawal of British troops from the six counties, and of its naval protection from the north-west approaches — he described it as 'a recipe for suicide'.[59]

3
THE BLITZ AND AFTER,
1941-1943

Death of Craig: Andrews Becomes Prime Minister

On 29 October 1940, Sir James Craig made his last major speech in
parliament — a typically impassioned tub-thumping assault on an opposition
motion supporting Irish unity. Almost four weeks later, on 24 November, he
died peacefully at his home. Lady Craigavon described her husband as having
been 'comfortable all through the day, reading and dozing'. They had listened
to the 6 o'clock news together on the wireless; she then left the room briefly
and on her return found that he 'had gone from her'.[1] It was a sign of the
times that the southern government's representative at his funeral, Senator
D.L. Robinson, should have felt it safer to travel up and down from Dublin
on the same day rather than stay overnight in Belfast. The public eulogies to
the late premier were predictably hagiographical. Spender's private
observations were much less fulsome and would no doubt have been concurred
with by much informed opinion. They reflected his deepening anxiety about
the inadequacy of recent unionist leadership and the resulting strains on
relations with Westminster. 'In later years', he wrote, '[Sir James's] health
prevented him from giving matters due attention ... [he gave] ... decisions or
advice to ministers across the water which ... [were] ... less than sound.
Death', he concluded, 'had thrown off all the weight of illness and cares
which had hung so heavily upon him during the last few years of his life'.[2]
He left a testing legacy for his successor, whose responsibility would be to
bring greater drive and direction to government and regain the full confidence
of Westminster.

After taking private soundings the Governor, Lord Abercorn, asked John
Andrews, the Minister of Finance, to form a government. He accepted but
informed the cabinet on 25 November that his agreement was contingent on
his being selected leader of the Unionist Party. Some informed opinion
regarded this condition as procedurally wrong and politically inept, as it
was likely to prejudice his authority during the critical early weeks of his

premiership. Nonetheless, the orderly transfer of power was regarded with a measure of relief, and Andrews' succession as inevitable and deserving, both on the grounds of his seniority and experience.

Andrews was born in 1871 at Comber, Co. Down of ancient Scottish dissenter stock. His family had an impressive record of success in business, (mainly high quality linen manufacture), but no tradition either of parliamentary representation or of military service. After attending school at Royal Belfast Academical Institution, he entered his father's firm and unashamedly championed the interests of local linen producers throughout his public life. He was ardently committed to free market capitalism but had a keen interest in labour questions and was sensitive and humane in his approach. Above all else, he was a fervent Unionist — active in the UUC and Orange Order from the 1900s and the party's MP for Mid-Down in the Belfast parliament from its foundation in May 1921. In the House, he was the most significant advocate and architect of 'step-by-step' with Britain's legislation and approach in social welfare matters. Until the end, he was an almost uncritical admirer of Craig, whom he regarded throughout as his party's indispensable leader. Though he was capable of a broader, more tolerant view than some of his colleagues, he was deeply suspicious of the south and of the northern minority. As a minister (at Labour 1921-37 and at Finance 1937-40) he largely compensated for his lack of charisma and flamboyance by his quiet diligence and dedication; he was trusted and liked by his cabinet colleagues and within the movement as a whole. From the late 1930s it was widely recognised that he shouldered the heaviest burden of government at Stormont. Apart from his departmental duties, he acted as premier during Craig's increasingly frequent absences and illnesses.

Despite this lifetime record of service, Andrews' appointment was greeted with resignation rather than enthusiasm. Sir James had resolutely refused to nominate a successor: when a close official adviser suggested that he ought to — in view of the growing risk of Luftwaffe attack — he declared 'I will never do that'.[3] At the time, Brooke betrayed no expectation at preferment or trace of disappointment.

Lord Craigavon (2nd from left) standing on the steps of Stormont beside John Andrews (2nd from right) who succeeded him in 1940
Public Record Office of Northern Ireland

Rather, he backed the new premier 'for all he is worth'[4] and along with Sir Wilfrid Spender stressed to him repeatedly the political necessity of making far-reaching cabinet changes. Unwisely, Andrews rejected this advice and retained the 'old guard'. Milne Barbour, who as Minister of Commerce was blamed for the persistently high levels of unemployment, was promoted to Finance. He was replaced at his old ministry by Brooke — an inspired choice. Just one new minister was appointed: in fulfilment of an earlier promise, Lord Glentoran, the gregarious Chief Whip, became Minister of Agriculture.

From the outset, it seemed unlikely that this reshuffled, rather than new, government would be capable of responding adequately to the pressures and challenges of war or of improving the often strained relations between London and Belfast. For several years, frustration and disillusionment had been mounting amongst unionist backbenchers, junior ministers and even within the party beyond Stormont. But as Herbert Shaw, in a report to the Foreign Office stated, hitherto 'no attempt at revolt could survive Lord Craigavon's frown'. He added, however, that Andrews was 'a much lesser man than his predecessor and [did] not enjoy anything like the same veneration amongst Ulster Unionists'.[5]

From its inception, Andrews' leadership appeared ineffectual and vulnerable. In late February 1941, his government lost its first by-election by 1,100 votes, on a 58% poll. It was held in North Down which was Craig's old seat. He had represented the county since 1906 and the constituency unopposed since 1921. The successful candidate, Independent Unionist and Alderman, T. Bailie, had been spoken of by his opponent, Major R. Workman, as though he was 'a member of the IRA and a menace to the security of Ulster, not to mention the Empire'.[6] Over the course of the next two years, backbench criticism tended to rise and the cabinet itself suffered from diminishing morale and growing fractiousness. Its hold on power became ever more enfeebled.

The Blitz

The new administration continued inauspiciously; neither its confidence nor its prestige were enhanced by the German air raids on Northern Ireland during April-May 1941. Too late, it had begun to appreciate that an aerial attack was likely and that if one did occur there was little hope of avoiding tragedy. Two months earlier Andrews was reportedly 'very concerned at our anti-aircraft defences' and at the 'position which might arise in Belfast after a severe air attack'.[7] Due in large part to earlier ministerial neglect and prevarication, local active and passive defences were hopelessly inadequate, and the public physically and psychologically unprepared for the blitz. In September 1940, both Belfast and Londonderry were provided with a light balloon barrage which was marginally reinforced six months later. By the spring of 1941, the strength of the anti-aircraft barrage in Northern Ireland had risen to 24 heavy guns and 14 light guns. Twenty-two of these were located in Belfast (6 light and 16 heavy). Four were sited at Londonderry (at Corrody and at Galliagh): more were to be transferred from Cardiff, but the Luftwaffe arrived before the guns did. Perhaps the most significant new development was the transfer, on 20 July 1940, from Turnhouse, near Edinburgh, to Aldergrove of a Royal Air Force squadron (No. 245) equipped with Hurricane fighters. Unfortunately these could only operate fully under daylight conditions. For 'certain technical reasons' (MacDermott's phrase)[8] experts predicted that any raid in force would be at night. There were no RAF fighters to defend Londonderry. Headquarters staff had moved into RAF Eglinton but the runways were incomplete; not until August 1941 did operational aircraft arrive. There were no searchlights in the province until 10 April 1941, though they had been recommended by imperial defence experts. Nor was there any provision for a smoke screen.

The government's other preparations were hardly reassuring, particularly after the Coventry attack (14 November 1940) when 50,000 houses were destroyed or damaged and 554 people died. In Belfast, for example, the shelters available could, if fully utilized, provide protection for just one quarter of the city's population. Its mortuary services had emergency plans to deal with only 200 bodies — a figure described by one official at the time as 'hardly enough'.[9] Finally, provision had been made for the care of a mere 10,000 people who might be made homeless as a consequence of future enemy action.

For Belfast, like Coventry, the word 'blitz' which is so evocative of sudden, terrifying, deadly aerial bombardment, was truly appropriate. In the course of four Luftwaffe attacks on the nights of 7-8 April, 15-16 April, 4-5 May and 5-6 May 1941, lasting ten hours in total, 1,100 people died, over 56,000 houses in the city were damaged (53% of its entire housing stock), roughly 100,000 made temporarily homeless and £20 million damage was caused to property at wartime values. It came twelfth in the 'league table' of urban areas attacked in the United Kingdom as measured by weight of bombs dropped. An ARP observer, Major Sean O'Sullivan, came up to Belfast from Dublin on the morning of Wednesday 16 April, hours after the first heavy raid had ended. He produced a detailed report for southern officials. It stated:

> In the Antrim Road and vicinity the attack was of a particularly concentrated character and in many instances bombs from successive waves of bombers fell within 15-20 yards of one another ... . In this general area, scores of houses were completely wrecked, either by explosion, fire or blast, while

hundreds were damaged so badly as to be uninhabitable ... . In suburban areas, many were allowed to burn themselves out and during the day wooden beams were still burning. ... During the night of 16-17, many of these smouldering fires broke out afresh and fire appliances could be heard passing throughout the night ... . It is estimated that the ultimate number of dead may be in the neighbourhood of 500, and final figures may even approach 2,000'. [The death toll was at least 900 and 600 were seriously injured.]

In the circumstances, O'Sullivan considered that the warden service ...'functioned efficiently. From the fact that some 200 incidents were reported from each of the two areas most affected, it must be concluded that [they] remained at their posts and reported damage promptly'. However, his opinion was that the whole civil defence sector was utterly overwhelmed. He continued:

The rescue service felt the want of heavy jacks, in one case the leg and arm of a child had to be amputated before it could be extricated ... [but] the greatest want appeared to be the lack of hospital facilities ... . At 2pm on the afternoon of the 16th (9 hours after the termination of the raid) it was reported that the street leading to the Mater Hospital was filled with ambulances waiting to set down their casualties ... Professor Flynn, head of the casualty service for the city, informed me that the greater number of casualties was due to shock, blast and secondary missiles, such as glass,

High Street, Belfast; the arrows indicate the areas on which the bombs fell
Public Record Office of Northern Ireland

stones, pieces of piping, etc.. There were many terrible mutilations among both living and dead — heads crushed, ghastly abdominal and face wounds, penetration by beams, mangled and crushed limbs etc ... . In the heavily 'blitzed' areas people ran panic-stricken into the streets and made for the open country. As many were caught in the open by blast and secondary missiles, the enormous number of casualties can be readily accounted for. It is perhaps true that many saved their lives running but I am afraid a much greater number lost them or became casualties ... . During the day, loosened slates and pieces of piping were falling in the streets and as pedestrians were numerous many casualties must have occurred.

The report concluded with the observation that 'A second Belfast would be too horrible to contemplate'.[10]

The city's mortuary services were also overwhelmed and as a result public baths (on the Falls Road and Peter's Hill) and a large fruit market (St. George's) had to be improvised to cope with the dead. Emma Duffin, who had served as a nurse near the western front during the first world war, was one of those on duty at St. George's market and she graphically recorded her impressions of the scene:

All the way to the place I had told myself I was bound to see horrible sights but only when seen could the full horror be realized. I had seen death in many forms, young men dying of ghastly wounds, but nothing I had ever seen was as terrible as this ... [World War I casualties] had died in hospital beds, their eyes had been reverently closed, their hands crossed to their breasts. Death had to a certain extent been ... made decent. It was solemn, tragic, dignified, but here it was grotesque, repulsive, horrible. No attendant nurse had soothed the last moments of these victims, no gentle reverent hand had closed their eyes or crossed their hands. With tangled hair, staring eyes, clutching hands, contorted limbs, their grey-green faces covered with dust, they lay, bundled into the coffins, half-shrouded in rugs or blankets, or an occasional sheet, still wearing their dirty, torn twisted garments. Death should be dignified, peaceful; Hitler had made even death grotesque. I felt outraged, I should have felt sympathy, grief, but instead feelings of revulsion and disgust assailed me.[11]

The official history says of this attack: 'Belfast was sorely tried, no other city in the United Kingdom, save London, had lost so many of her citizens in one night's raid. No other city, except possibly Liverpool, ever did'.[12] In fact, John Maffey, who passed through Belfast on the morning after the first raid, informed the Irish government that the scenes he witnessed there were 'more horrifying than London because of the numbers of small dwelling houses of poor people which were destroyed.'[13] Also, in Dublin the German Minister, Eduard Hempel, felt constrained to call by appointment (on the morning of 17 April) with the Irish Minister of External Affairs, J.P. Walshe, to offer sympathy and attempt an explanation. Walshe recorded that the German was 'clearly distressed by the news of the severe raid on Belfast and especially of the number of civilian casualties'. He stated that 'he would once more tell his government how he felt about the matter and he would ask them to confine the operations to military objectives as far as it was humanly possible. He believed that this was being done already but it was inevitable that a certain number of civilian lives should be lost in the course of heavy bombing from the air'.[14]

However, a further severe raid followed on the night of 4-5 May (the 'fire-raid'). During the course of 3° hours, roughly 100,000 incendiary bombs were dropped, followed by high explosives, from an estimated 200 aircraft, mainly on central, north and east Belfast. The resulting fires were on a scale beyond the resources of local brigades within the first sixty minutes. Over

High Street after the Luftwaffe attack, 4-5 May 1941
Public Record Office of Northern Ireland

200 buildings were ablaze by the time of the 'all clear'. The death rate was lower than during the Easter Tuesday attack, but unidentified bodies were once again brought to St. George's market. The key strategic industries sustained very heavy damage. No British shipyard suffered greater physical destruction during a single raid than did Harland & Wolff on this occasion. On the morning after the attack, Emma Duffin noted 'the smell of burning was in the air. The grass was strewn with blackened and charred papers. There was a sheet from a child's essay book. On the top of the page I read *The End of the World*. It seemed appropriate. It was the end of the world as we knew it'.[15] As in mid-April, help in fighting fires and in rescue work was provided by the troops based locally and more was requested from all over Northern Ireland, from Britain, and from Eire. By responding, the south thereby compromised its policy of neutrality and risked becoming a target itself. When war had broken out, Ribbentrop had menacingly informed de Valera that Germany would refrain from hostile action if Ireland maintained an unimpeachable policy of neutrality towards her.

After the first severe attack, William D. Scott, permanent secretary of the Ministry of Commerce, advised Andrews that he should make a personal appeal emphasizing that 'our best reply ... is redoubled effort'. He quoted as a possible source of inspiration an extract from Abraham Lincoln's Gettysburg Address: 'It is for us the living, rather, to be dedicated here to the unfinished work'.[16] Its sentiments if not its eloquence are discernible in Andrews' subsequent press statements. In fact, fear and panic had already reached epidemic proportions, especially in Belfast. O'Sullivan observed after the Easter Tuesday raid:

> From the early morning of the 16th and all throughout the day there was a continuous 'trek' to railway stations. The refugees looked dazed and horror-stricken and many had neglected to bring more than a few belongings — I saw one man with just an extra pair of socks stuck in his pockets. Any and every means of exit from the city was availed of and the final destination appeared to be a matter of indifference. Train after train and bus after bus were filled with those next in line. At nightfall the Northern Counties Station [in York Street] was packed from platform gates to entrance gates and still refugees were coming along in a steady stream from the surrounding streets ... Open military lorries were finally put into service and even expectant mothers and mothers with young children were put into these in the rather heavy drizzle that lasted throughout the evening. On the 17th I heard that hundreds who either could not get away or could not leave for other reasons simply went out into the fields and remained in the open all night with whatever they could take in the way of covering.[17]

That same day Moya Woodside noted in her diary:

Evacuation is taking on panic proportions. Roads out of town are still one stream of cars, with mattresses and bedding tied on top. Everything on wheels is being pressed into service. People are leaving from all parts of town and not only from the bombed areas. Where they are going, what they will find to eat when they get there, nobody knows. This business presents a problem of the first proportions to Stormont.[18]

The condition of those fleeing from the city shocked Woodside as much as did their numbers. She reported that:

My mother telephoned to say that she took in 8 evacuees last night, 2 mothers and 6 children. Says one mother is about to have another baby any minute, that they are all filthy, the smell in the room is terrible. They refuse all food except bread and tea; the children have made puddles all over the floor etc. She is terribly sorry for them and kindliness itself but finds this relevation of how the other half live rather overpowering.

The next day, she continued,

Belfast slum dwellers are pretty far down and to those not used to seeing poverty and misery at close quarters the effect is overwhelming. 'The smell is terrible', said my sister-in-law. 'They don't even use the lavatories, they just do it on the floor, grown-ups and children'. She said she had been given the job of finding private billets for the evacuees and she was ashamed to have to ask decent working people with clean houses to take in such guests. More are 'scared out' than 'bombed out', too.[19]

After the May raids the assessment given in the German media that Belfast's industry had been devastated beyond recovery would have been widely accepted within the city itself. Morale all but collapsed. A Ministry of Home Affairs' report estimated that by the end of that month as many as 220,000 persons had temporarily fled from the capital. They scattered through Ulster and beyond. They arrived in Fermanagh having 'nothing with them only night shirts';[20] 10,000 crossed the border. Superimposed on the massive British military presence, available accommodation was stretched beyond its limits. Dawson Bates had to inform cabinet of the rack-renting of barns, and in some areas of up to 30 people crowded together in small houses. Even in early August Moya Woodside described a 'friend whose car broke down ... in a tiny seaside village'. She continued: 'The food situation is alarming. He could not find ... anywhere to stay the night and had to sleep out in the sandhills ... He was unable to get anything to eat ... even of tea and bread. Village shops were completely sold out'. Three weeks earlier, she herself visited a family in Belfast which was 'paying the full rent for a house of which the two upper rooms were quite uninhabitable, the downstairs windows covered with felt, and the gas supply cut off. All cooking had to be done in semi-darkness over an open fire'. It was 'little more than a shelter. Yet there is competition even to get these'. Thousands of those remaining in the city 'ditched'; during the hours of darkness they streamed ('trekked') along the main arterial roads to the suburbs, to shelter in parks, ditches and hedgerows, until first light when they felt it safe to return. The scale of continuing public fear was highlighted when, after an air-raid alert on 23 July 1941, at 2.00am, an estimated 30,000 fled from the city in motor vehicles, bicycles and on foot; an eye- witness likened it to 'the crowds at a football match'.[21] No aircraft appeared and no bombs fell.

Police reports indicate that 'ditching' became a feature not only of contemporary life in Belfast but also of the province's larger county towns. The habit was spread by evacuees after the city had been blitzed. Also on Easter Tuesday night (15-16 April) a number of bombing incidents occurred elsewhere in the province, scattered along the Luftwaffe's flight path. In the most serious of these the same features which had characterised the experience of the capital were paralleled though on an infinitely smaller scale — most of the bombs fell on residential property, the public was unprotected and unprepared, active defences were inadequate, blackout measures defective and the few shelters available under-utilized.

No provincial city or town suffered more than Londonderry. This was not unexpected. It had experienced its first air raid alert on 25 October 1940. After the fall of France, its port rapidly emerged as a vital base for the protection of the western approaches, and it had also developed into a significant centre of ship construction and repair. MacDermott had, for several months, been concerned that its defences had failed to keep pace with its evolving strategic and industrial role. During one of his broadcasts, William Joyce (Lord Haw-Haw), identified the naval base as a prospective target and referred to the British Army 'hiding behind the golden teapot in Derry'.[22] It seems likely that he was referring to the presence of allied ships sheltering in the port, roughly opposite Waterloo Place, where a large hanging ornamental teapot adorned McCullagh's teahouse. On 15 March, *The Londonderry Sentinel* warned its readers of the dangers of complacency: '[We hope] to escape the attention of the Nazi airmen throughout the war ... our immunity hitherto may well prove our greatest peril because of the false sense of security it gives'.

Shortly after midnight on Easter Tuesday night, two large parachute mines were dropped from 8,000 feet probably by a single bomber and landed near ex-servicemen's homes in Messines Park. Five houses were demolished,

15 people killed (all of them members of ex-servicemen's families) and 150 made homeless, at least temporarily. It remains unclear whether the attack was indiscriminate, or if the objective had been to disrupt the port by blocking the river Foyle or, more likely, to damage the naval yard at Pennyburn, 3-500 yards away. Such was its impact that many people subsequently 'trekked' to the outskirts of the city at night, and slept in ditches and tents. Others travelled to Buncrana every evening in what became known as 'the blitz

The variety of warships berthed along the quayside, Londonderry, at the height of the Battle of the Atlantic *Ian Mullen*

train'.[23] Approximately one hour later (on the night of 15-16 April) two other urban areas nearer Belfast also suffered. At about 1.00am Newtownards airport (Co. Down) was struck; ten guards were killed and a number of civilians injured. Simultaneously, six miles away, Bangor was attacked. Fourteen bombing incidents were reported, in which five civilians died and 35 were injured. In this quiet seaside town, there was no obvious strategic target for the raid.

Overall the blitz exacerbated the government's problems, confirmed its directionless, hesitant posture and lessened still further its residual popularity. In late May MacDermott even raised with Spender the possibility that public anger over the lack of local preparation for Luftwaffe attack, and the inadequacy of Northern Ireland's defences might result in an assault by irate mobs on the parliament buildings at Stormont. It did not materialize. However, within the Commons chamber, the minister was the butt of very bitter verbal attacks from backbenchers. In an attempt to mollify them, he addressed a party meeting on civil defence and the cabinet reluctantly agreed to a parliamentary demand for a secret session.

May 1941 – Conscription?

In addition, the province's experience of the blitz contributed to the re-opening of the conscription question. It had lain dormant for almost two years. In mid-May, MacDermott passionately advocated its introduction, stating that otherwise 'he would not be able to carry on'.[24] He regarded it as the essential means of restoring public discipline and of achieving equality of sacrifice. Levels of voluntary recruitment had remained modest, and in some areas the civil defence services continued to experience difficulty in attracting sufficient personnel. The Governor, Lord Abercorn, was likewise strongly in favour and encouraged Andrews to 'strike when people's feelings are hot'.[25] There is some evidence that the public mood might possibly have been favourable. Harry Midgley, a leading Labour politician, anticipated that implementation would cause no 'trouble in the shipyard because the recent bombings had brought the workers much closer together'.[26] In similar vein, Moya Woodside noted that 'bombs [had] fallen on Catholics and Protestants alike' and that nationalist opinion 'if not pro-British [was] at least much less pro-German'.[27]

Meanwhile, quite independently, on 12 May 1941, Ernest Bevin the Minister of Labour at Westminster, suggested to the imperial war cabinet that the extension of conscription to Northern Ireland deserved 'further consideration',[28] given the accumulating shortage of manpower in Britain. Both he and Churchill were especially enthusiastic about its implementation. It was estimated that, if applied, some 48-53,000 men could be raised. During the subsequent inter-governmental negotiations held at Westminster on Saturday 24 May, the response of the Stormont ministers present was unequivocally and uniformly enthusiastic. (Andrews was accompanied by Brooke, MacDermott, Glentoran and Gordon).

Nonetheless, three days later, on 27 May, the British government publicly declared that conscription would not, after all, be introduced into the six counties. This was due to accumulating evidence of opposition to the proposal. De Valera stated that it would be 'an act of oppression ... It revolts the human conscience'.[29] There was protest also from sections of opinion in the United States and Canada, and crucially from within Northern Ireland itself. When Herbert Morrison asked Charles Wickham for his views on the likely impact of its introduction into the north, he predicted massive resistance. He pointed out, in a detailed memorandum, that a substantial proportion of those called up would be Catholics (as so many Protestants were employed in reserved occupations) who would take their lead from the Hierarchy and it had utterly condemned the proposal. In nationalist areas, he anticipated that large numbers of men would seek to escape the draft by crossing the border (Churchill's response was that 'no obstacle would be placed in the way of those running away').[30] He feared also clashes in the streets with the RUC, arrests, hunger strikes and gun battles. He believed that the IRA (then estimated by the Home Office to be 2,000 strong) would be given a new lease of life. Wickham's testimony was likely to have been influential, as British intelligence regarded him as 'particularly well informed and astute'.[31] Herbert Morrison similarly expected that its introduction would cause a renewal of strife between protestant and catholic workmen with 'disorder in the shipyard and other places'. If proceeded with, he advised that the 'government must be prepared to deal with large scale resistance' even to the point of setting up 'concentration camps for thousands of resistors'.[32] Dublin ministers also predicted 'bloodshed among the nationalist population' and 'trouble of all kinds between Nationalists and Orangemen'.[33]

Meanwhile, evidence of the accuracy of these sombre predictions was already emerging in the province. Nationalist MPs and Senators, actively supported by the Roman Catholic Hierarchy, orchestrated a province-wide anti-conscription campaign, culminating in a mass rally held in Belfast on Sunday, 25 May. It was attended by up to 10,000 people and so impressed Andrews that next morning, solely on his own initiative, he contacted the Home Office. He stated that the level of resistance would be greater than he had earlier anticipated and though his government favoured its application, 'the real test ... must be whether it would be for the good of the Empire'.[34] This was also likely to have influenced the war cabinet when, next day, it agreed a statement later cheered at Westminster, which concluded that it 'would be more trouble than it was worth'.[35]

The preceding policy vacillations of the Stormont administration can only have served to reduce its credibility at Westminster and to raise further doubts about the quality of its leadership. Bevin complained that Northern

Ireland was 'asking for a privileged position'; it was seeking munitions contracts when 'we had not had conscription and that was the fault of ... [the Ulster] government. We had got cold feet'.[36] Moreover, within the province itself the unionist leadership had failed to implement its publicly stated policy, and its nationalist opponents could legitimately claim a victory. Wickham was convinced, however, that conscription would not have had wholehearted protestant support either. Woodside noted that the final outcome was 'welcomed by most, except ardent Unionists'.[37] There can be little doubt that it was also in the best interests of public order. Moreover, between September 1941-May 1945, 11,500 persons from the six counties volunteered for service and 18,600 Eire recruits were formally approved in the Northern Ireland recruiting area; the implementation of conscription would indeed therefore have been 'more trouble than it was worth'.

The Government's Falling Popularity

By the autumn of 1941, Andrews was convinced that his political position had become stronger. By then, the province had partially recovered from the disruption of the blitz. Most of Belfast's evacuees had returned from the countryside; boredom, the inconvenience of living outside the city, the termination of Luftwaffe attacks on British cities from late May and the German invasion of Russia on 22 June contributed to their return. Meanwhile, perhaps surprisingly, unemployment had fallen sharply from the beginning of the year. The government's second by-election defeat, however, on 3 December 1941, shattered the Prime Minister's cosy but inaccurate assumption. It took place in the Belfast constituency of Willowfield; it had a predominantly protestant skilled working-class electorate and had voted solidly unionist since its creation.[38] Harry Midgley stood as Labour candidate. His brand of politics was 'suddenly viewed in a less hostile light' after Hitler had launched his attack on the USSR. He also benefited from the measurable war-time swing to the left already evident elsewhere in the United Kingdom. On the question of Northern Ireland's position within the union, he spoke reassuringly, stating that 'there could not be and must not be'[39] any alteration without the consent of the Ulster people. This commitment was vital to his prospects. His opponent, F.J. Lavery, nonetheless sought to promote the partition issue. He was an uninspiring choice and does not appear to have enjoyed much personal popularity even among Unionists. The *Belfast Telegraph* suggested that Midgley's victory (by 4,774 votes) was partly 'because the Unionist Party machine rates public intelligence too low when it expects the border issue and any candidate to be sufficient at the present time to ensure an official victory'.[40] The result has been described as 'indisputably the biggest electoral upset in Northern Ireland politics since the state's formation'.[41]

Belfast Corporation Suspended

For Andrews the outcome was both a shock and a disappointment. Soon afterwards he expressed privately his concern that in a general election his government would lose its Commons majority. A number of senior colleagues shared this anxiety. Awareness of their vulnerability reinforced their cautious, conservative instincts. Over the next two years they provided ever more inconsistent and indecisive leadership. They sought to postpone subsequent by-elections and made more determined efforts to avoid contentious policies or unpopular legislation, even to the extent of deferring salary increases for the civil service. Some politically hazardous issues, however, demanded their attention. Amongst these were the much-publicised activities of Belfast Corporation.

The 75 local authorities which the province's government inherited in 1921 had been a constant source of political controversy and tension. Initially, the refusal of a number of those under nationalist control to recognise the Belfast parliament had led to their suspension and contributed, in 1922, to the abolition of Proportional Representation in council elections and the associated gerrymandering of electoral boundaries. Subsequently, frequent quarrels between the two tiers of government continued to arise — over matters of finance and the failure of some authorities to fulfil their responsibilities adequately or honestly. Spender was scathing in his condemnation of them. He was convinced that 'lower elements ... associated with the local authorities' were intent on gaining 'control of the [Unionist] party machine' and believed that it would be 'very difficult to rid [it]... of the dirt that [had] crept in'.[42]

A Home Affairs inquiry into Whiteabbey Sanitorium (issued 15 June 1941) indicated that Belfast Corporation had been guilty of wide-ranging corruption and abuse of patronage as well as 'gross neglect' and incompetence ('complete laxity'). As a result, a growing proportion of the city's ratepayers favoured its dissolution. The cabinet's position was an extremely delicate one, as the councillors were predominantly unionist and had considerable influence both within the Belfast associations and inside the broader organisation as well. (The party's headquarters in Glengall Street had for some time been aware of the emergence of a 'City Hall party' and 'discerned in it an alternative focus of power'.)[43]

Initially the cabinet nurtured the forlorn hope that the Corporation might be induced to reform itself. In due course, its members appointed a committee which produced a report but its recommendations were rejected by the council on 2 April 1942. After this failure, Dawson Bates, the minister responsible, recommended that, as a compromise, administrators should be appointed who would act as an executive for the borough but be guided by the elected council. He advised his government colleagues, on 20 April, that if more punitive action (such as outright dissolution) was taken, they would in his opinion find it 'impossible to hold office'.[44]

Even this modest proposal was adopted by some ministers with extreme reluctance. Andrews especially was anxious 'not to have any trouble with the corporation' or, as he explained unconvincingly to his cabinet (on 8 June 1942) to 'detract from the unity of effort ... needed to win the war'.[45] Under powerful pressure from both the city's councillors and some of its unionist branches, a majority in the government therefore agreed to adopt two amendments which weakened further the measure (the County Borough Administration Bill) which Bates had proposed. The first specified the precise period for which city administrators would be appointed, and the second restored to the council some of its powers to make appointments. However, the latter was criticised by opposition MPs (Midgley in particular) with such devastating effect that it was hurriedly withdrawn. The legislation which was finally adopted provided for the appointment of three administrators for a three and a half-year period and they were empowered to 'make all appointments, purchases, contracts and rates and municipal taxes'. They proceeded to govern the city with 'quiet efficiency'[46] with the assistance of a civil servant from Stormont. Nevertheless the episode deepened divisions within the government and within the broader party: some members regarded this response as insufficiently punitive while others thought it too severe.

Industrial Unrest

The government's handling of industrial unrest was another unavoidable aspect of its wartime responsibilities which raised further doubts about its competence and provoked adverse comment from British ministers and officials, as well as within Northern Ireland itself. In part, public censure was directed at the official machinery for resolving trade disputes. Even John MacDermott, Attorney General (from November 1941) described it as 'clumsy and slow' adding that it thus 'tempted' workers to 'take matters into their own hands'.[47]

A much more damaging criticism, expressed strongly by sections of local management, some high-ranking civil servants in Stormont and the British Ministry of Labour and National Service was that the Northern Ireland cabinet was weak and inconsistent in its dealings with labour. It was suggested that this had served to undermine workers' morale and so contributed to a deterioration in industrial discipline. W.P. Kemp, the director at Short & Harland's aircraft factory, complained in late September 1942 that refractory workers knew that their actions would be 'winked at by those in authority' and that this had encouraged 'mob rule'.[48] During the following month, the worst strike of Andrews' premiership erupted. It originated in a Shorts dispersal plant at Balmoral, Belfast. Within two weeks it had spread and was affecting 10,000 men in the city's major strategic industries (aircraft, shipbuilding and engineering). It prompted Churchill to express his 'shock at what [was] happening'.[49] It was eventually ended after direct intervention by British trade union leaders, invited over by Stormont ministers. The dispute had arisen out of an attempt by management to enforce a Ministry of Production instruction regarding Sunday work. Its root causes were complex but inevitably much blame attached to the role of the government. Westminster officials considered that it showed 'deplorable weakness'[50] during the strike. Locally, it was also castigated for its 'general policy of drift'.[51]

By November 1942, MacDermott had become acutely despondent about the government's entire approach to labour relations. Accordingly, he suggested to Andrews that the order making it an offence to strike should be repealed, as it clearly did nothing to deter mass industrial action and consequently threatened to bring the whole rule of law into disrepute. Once more he strongly advocated conscription. He suggested that 'the strain of war [was] likely to increase', adding forlornly, 'I doubt if we as a community have the discipline or sense of responsibility to meet it without further trouble'.[52] Shortly afterwards on 11 April 1943, Churchill likewise reopened the issue.

He appealed directly to the American President, F.D. Roosevelt (who had opposed its introduction in 1941) outlining the deleterious effects of not applying conscription. He described how, in Northern Ireland, 'young fellows of the locality ... loaf about with their hands in their pockets', and suggested that their presence had a negative impact 'not only [on] recruiting, but the work of ... Belfast Shipyard which is less active than other British shipyards'.[53] Andrews was not impressed by arguments projecting the proposal as a panacea for labour indiscipline, poor productivity or the disappointing level of voluntary recruitment. He stated tersely that it did not fall within the realm of 'practical' politics.[54] Meanwhile the government's machinery for dealing with industrial unrest and its approach to labour problems remained unchanged. So too did the tensions within the cabinet and the criticism of its performance which these circumstances engendered.

Looking to the Future

To many the government appeared to be not just incompetent, but also lethargic in its response to the changing mood of the electorate. Nevertheless, there was a more positive, even if no more convincing, aspect to the policies of Andrews and his cabinet. Immediately after taking office, the new premier became noticeably more enthusiastic about raising public expenditure on social services, setting aside more resources for post-war reconstruction and asserting more forcefully his government's independence of Treasury control. Indeed, leading officials at Stormont were surprised by his sudden enthusiasm for increased spending and struck by the contrast between his views as Prime Minister and his more penny-pinching approach as Minister of Finance. Spender dismissed the transformation as a crude attempt to buy votes or, in his own phrase, 'at getting credit from the electorate by the distribution of government funds'.[55] He also suspected that the premier sought better terms for the province than were available in Britain and regarded this as unjustifiable and damaging to Northern Ireland's reputation. This suspicion was shared by Basil Brooke and influential junior ministers and it contributed to the overall uneasiness at the unpredictable nature of Andrews' leadership.

It was certainly the case that Andrews expressed his support for increased government spending more stridently as he became more aware of the political weakness of his administration and of the shifting aspirations of the Northern Ireland people. In wartime, the border issue inevitably receded and there was mounting popular interest in post-war planning — to raise standards in health, housing and education and to forestall any return to the unemployment and distress of the 'hungry 30s'. The squalid condition of the blitz evacuees from Belfast heightened popular awareness of the appalling scale and depth of poverty and increased consciousness of the inadequacy of local welfare provision compared with Great Britain. John Oliver was one of the civil servants who directed the evacuation. One of his colleagues wryly penned their reaction:

> They wept like anything to see
> Such quantities of fleas
> Such lousy little Protestants,
> Such nitty young RCs[56]

A clergyman, Rev. J.B. Woodburn, a former Moderator of the Presbyterian Church, who had worked in the city for 19 years, wrote on 2 June 1941: 'I never saw the like of them before ... wretched people, very undersized and underfed, down and out looking men and women ... Is it credible to us that there should be such people in a Christian country? If something is not done now, to remedy this rank inequality, there will be a revolution after the war'.[57]

High wartime taxation and the province's huge imperial contribution (it rose from £1.3 million to £36.3 million between 1939-45) suggested that the government had the means to respond positively; all that it required was the will.

Westminster's publication of the Beveridge report in 1942 fuelled expectations of reform. William Beveridge was an egotistical, vain academic and wartime civil servant, but publication of his drearily entitled 'Social Insurance and the Allied Services' transformed him overnight into a national celebrity and soon afterwards an MP. It outsold any British Stationery Office document until the Denning report on the Profumo affair in 1963. It identified the five 'giant' evils of pre-war society — Want, Disease, Ignorance, Squalor and Idleness — and advocated the means whereby they might be eradicated. These expanded on earlier reform measures and included a comprehensive system of national insurance, a scheme of national assistance, family allowances and a national health service.

Within Northern Ireland, the press gave the report moderate coverage and certainly Unionists such as Spender had deep reservations about Beveridge's main proposals, in particular their financial feasibility. Nonetheless it was not long in being absorbed into the local political culture. Harry Midgley's newly-formed Commonwealth Party gave it total and instant support; it reinforced his commitment to the union. Irish unity, he argued, would 'destroy for many years to come the expectation (created by the possibility of the Beveridge scheme) of an enlarged and expanded system of social security'.[58] Broadly at least the unionist leadership had come to the conclusion by 1943, that not to implement it fully would be 'to commit political suicide'.[59] From an early stage in the war, more politically astute elements within the party were deeply concerned about the wartime 'drift to the left'. In 1939 its leadership had decided to abandon political activity, regarding it as a distraction from the war effort. In 1941, this decision had to be reversed in view of the alarming advances being made by the labour movement. Nevertheless, Midgley's electoral success in December suggested that its progress was continuing. In 1943, the *News Letter* expressed concern at the spread of socialism among working people. In 1944 Tom Harrisson likewise noted that the Labour Party was 'emerging strongly', adding that its 'poll cuts across the religious divide for the first time'.[60]

Against this background — the border issue eclipsed, growing social awareness due mainly to the blitz and the Beveridge report, Ulster's soaring imperial contribution and the measureable 'drift to the left' — some Unionists pressed the Prime Minister to react decisively. In mid-1942, a group of junior ministers and a high-ranking party official urged upon him the absolute necessity of responding positively, by formulating comprehensive plans for the post-war years. They suggested that this should be done as 'publicly and speedily as possible'. This they considered would 'arouse enthusiasm and capture the imagination of a great majority of the people' and was 'essential for the future of the province as well as of the party'.[61] Andrews' sympathetic response stemmed from conviction as much as political calculation. He fully shared public concern at the inadequacy of local health, housing and educational provision, the nature and level of poor relief and the extent to which the six counties lagged behind the standards of social welfare attained in Britain. He was himself convinced that over the years the imperial government had failed to treat the province equitably and expressed privately his mounting frustration at the constraints imposed by Westminster on his government's proposed expenditure.

The tangible outcome of these discreet, though firm, pressures was both meagre and contentious. The Prime Minister made a detailed statement at Stormont on post-war policy, delivering it on 30 July 1942, the eve of the summer recess. This effectively denied the House an opportunity to discuss its contents until the following September. Andrews' speech contained a strong commitment to improvements in a wide range of social services (including housing, electricity and education) and referred in some detail to future plans for transport, local government and industry. It immediately provoked an angry response from Kingsley Wood, the Chancellor of the Exchequer, and from Treasury officials. In correspondence and in later discussions, they criticised the entire absence of consultation preceding the speech, particularly as they regarded 'parity of social services as the sheet anchor of ... [their] ... financial relations with the province'.[62] Its timing they regarded as incomprehensible, and its content as unwisely specific. They stressed that the post-war period might well be one of hardship, shortages and high taxation, and thus to suggest that plans would be ready for immediate implementation was misleading. The statement was variously described by the Treasury mandarins as a crude 'attempt to bolster up his [Andrews'] political position by promising the moon', a 'dangerous lapse into the "homes for heroes" tone ... we were to eschew this time' and a bid to establish the principle that 'whatever tune Northern Ireland calls the Imperial government will pay the piper'.[63]

In the course of these exchanges, Wood recognised that the major responsibility for post-war planning in Northern Ireland lay with the regional government. But he also stressed that, though it might legitimately exercise the right to make up 'leeway' with Britain in its social services, it could not claim preferential treatment. Andrews deduced from this that he had gained 'extended financial powers ... from before'.[64] This favourable interpretation was not shared by Treasury or Ministry of Finance officials or by Maynard Sinclair, the parliamentary secretary at Finance. Spender more acutely observed that the Chancellor's letter merely 'confirmed existing arrangements'.[65] He was coming to the view that Sir Basil Brooke, then Minister of Commerce, was a 'man who would govern more responsibly'.[66]

In the meantime, the governmental machinery for post-war reconstruction established at Stormont by the Prime Minister had degenerated (in Brooke's phrase) into a 'hopeless muddle'[67] of overlapping and competing committees, struggling without success to devise coherent plans for the post-war years. Not surprisingly, when the question was eventually debated in the House (on 20 October 1942), a number of backbenchers expressed strong reservations regarding Andrews' ability to fulfil the promises made in his earlier Commons statement. His claim that he would apply 'foresight, energy and courage'[68] to resolve peacetime problems seemed hollow and unconvincing. On 18 January 1943, even the *Belfast News Letter* reflected ruefully on 'how little thought seems to have been given to the political future'.

The Economy Improving

Meanwhile, the only consolation for the government was the consistently impressive record of Northern Ireland agriculture and the recent decline in the rate of unemployment. It had begun to drop in late 1941 (then 70,000); by June of that year it had fallen by 20,000 despite the blitz. And by April 1943, just 18,896 persons (5% of the insured labour force) were without work. This relative improvement was due to a combination of factors. Voluntary enlistment, even on a modest level, and the migration of labour to British munitions factories had a cumulative effect. By 1942, 40,000 workers had transferred to Great Britain, though an unknown number returned, especially, a Home Office official observed acidly, 'if bombs fell in their vicinity whilst over here'.[69] In addition, the building of shelters and of bases and airfields for British and later American troops created jobs in the construction industry. (The British government gave Stormont clear instructions that the latter was to be regarded as the greater priority.) Also more contracts were placed with local firms as those elsewhere in the United Kingdom reached full capacity. These improving opportunities were skilfully exploited by Ministry of Commerce officials and by Sir Basil Brooke, its head. He took every advantage of his social contacts at Westminster in his search for orders, sought to improve inter-governmental liaison and ensured that Northern Ireland producers were on the lists kept by British supply departments and so received their fair allocation of war work. He sought as well to make the province a more attractive option to UK ministers. Threatening resignation, he insisted that Belfast electricity generating capacity was dispersed to locations outside the strategically vulnerable harbour estate. He strove to improve the unsatisfactory production record of leading heavy manufacturers in the city — by personally visiting factories, by publicity to instil a greater sense of war urgency (one ministry slogan was 'Have you declared war on Hitler?'),[70] by changing managerial structures and by initiatives to improve labour relations and to ensure that skilled workers were utilised to optimum effect.

Brooke's close identification with the war effort, his sense of urgency and his ministerial competence were widely recognised and commented upon by unionist backbenchers and junior ministers. They compared his performance favourably with that of his cabinet colleagues. The significance of their comments was more than merely transitory; their attitudes and actions from January 1943 largely determined the fate of the Andrews' government and finally propelled Brooke to the premiership.

Andrews' Fall

Overall, there seemed no shortage of evidence to confirm the collective incompetence of the 'old guard' whether in the lack of preparation for the blitz, the persistently high levels of unemployment relative to those in Britain, the mishandling of the conscription issue and, it was alleged, labour matters or the confusion over post-war planning. These features had also placed additional strain on relations with Westminster. In his maiden speech, Midgley charged 'the government with presenting a poor image of Northern Ireland to the people of Britain'.[71] There was still much truth in MacDermott's jibe that the region appeared to be 'only half in the war'.[72] This impression struck informed British observers even more forcefully. Though the ultimate responsibility for some of the province's distinct and unenviable characteristics undoubtedly lay with Westminster rather than Stormont, a growing and influential sector of local opinion attributed them to the failings of Andrews and his colleagues.

By January 1943, Spender had become convinced of the need for cabinet change. In his view, Andrews and his government had fostered complacency and, unlike Carson in the Great War, had failed lamentably to offer 'leadership and sacrifice'.[73] In early 1943, however, any revolt which might seriously threaten the survival of Andrews' administration seemed highly improbable. Out of 39 government supporters in the House, 16 held offices of profit under the crown and the total number of private members had been depleted by military service. Moreover, there was a dearth of decisive leadership amongst unionist backbenchers capable of articulating their frustration or mobilizing their voting strength (the Stormont parliament had been consistently amateurish, ill-informed and lacking in authority). Yet there are clear indications that dissension within the party was growing. Parliamentary party meetings had gradually become more tense with, on occasion, even routine business, such as the filling of vacant seats in the Senate, leading to acrimonious debate and resentment. As a result, ministers were more reluctant to meet members. This reticence was used by critics to justify moving hostile private motions in the House on the grounds that they were being denied any alternative means of ventilating their grievances.

The extent of parliamentary disaffection was starkly revealed on 9-10 January 1943 when unionist backbenchers held a secret meeting at which they formulated demands, later forwarded to the Chief Whip. They called both for a change of leadership and the immediate appointment of younger ministers. Their action was as much a symptom as a cause of political crisis. The *Belfast News Letter*, which was sympathetic to Andrews, described it as 'a reflection of a widespread feeling in the constituencies of which the last ... by-election gave unmistakable evidence'.[74] There was widespread contemporary recognition amongst senior party members and officials and leading civil servants that the public had lost confidence in the government. Even before the MPs had met, a group of junior ministers had privately indicated their support not just for a reshuffling of the cabinet but for the removal of Andrews himself and had actively been considering resignation. They had come to regard him as the source of the administration's ineffectiveness and his continuation in office as a threat to the preservation of law and order, to party unity and even democracy itself, and the union — given the strained relations with Westminster. After hearing the backbenchers' proposals, Brooke noted privately that the Prime Minister ought to 'retire at once', adding that it was 'difficult for any of us to remain'.[75]

Somewhat surprisingly, given his government's consistently conciliatory, even weak, record, Andrews' own response was to resist the malcontents and to defend himself and his ministers. He entirely under-estimated the gravity of the challenge; he was quoted in the press as saying 'I don't look worried, do I?'[76] However, at a party meeting held to discuss the crisis on 19 January eight speakers (including three junior ministers) called for a 'new team' and a 'change of leadership' if electoral disaster was to be avoided. The Prime Minister spoke for 30 minutes strongly in defence of the *status quo*. Despite this, a resolution was then passed unanimously, affirming that the 'subject requires careful ... consideration' and that he 'should not be asked to make a further statement on the matter until a party meeting is convened by him for the purpose'.[77]

It was now generally assumed that Andrews would at least make changes in his cabinet; Brooke advised him to do so on at least four occasions over the next four weeks. However, informed sources were soon reporting that his attitude had in fact stiffened. This was soon evident from his efforts to rouse support for his government through a series of public speeches delivered around the province and from the expansive content of the King's Speech.

There was speculation that he would appeal for backing at the Ulster Unionist Council's annual conference. Spender also noted that he was 'anxious to put forward a lot of names for political honours'[78] and claimed that this bait had helped influence the attitude of one of Belfast's morning newspapers. On 23 February the Prime Minister instructed the parliamentary party, just returned for a new session of the Commons, that no decision regarding ministerial changes could be made before Easter. This prevarication served to confirm doubts as to his suitability for leadership.

At a further party meeting held on 19 March, Andrews stated categorically that he would not tolerate interference in his selection of ministers and he reaffirmed his opinion that his government colleagues were the best available. A vote of confidence in the premier was then moved, challenged and reluctantly withdrawn. A second resolution passed unanimously: it requested that the Prime Minister 'reconsider the question of changes in his cabinet'.[79] The three-hour proceedings were concluded, for the first time in 22 years of parliamentary party meetings, by a rendering of the national anthem. This was a vain attempt to recapture a lost unity.

When the UUC met on 16 April, it passed by acclamation a resolution of unabated confidence in Andrews' leadership, though only after some 'pretty hot speeches'.[80] He later stressed to Churchill that out of 750 delegates just two or three had dissented. He possibly now believed that the crisis would pass — given this success, the expressions of support he had recently received from a number of local associations and the assumed backing of a majority of the party at Stormont. During his statement to the Council, however, he had again implied that he would not make any cabinet changes. As a result, at least three junior ministers were 'eager to push in their resignations right away' (Brian Maginess, Maynard Sinclair and Dehra Parker). On reflection, they decided to delay until the next party meeting. This was eventually arranged by the leadership, under duress, for 28 April. Meanwhile Brooke placed his resignation in Andrews' hands so that he would 'have an opportunity to speak'.[81]

Amidst rumours of mass resignations from the government, 33 Unionist MPs assembled at party headquarters, Glengall Street, each pledged to secrecy regarding the proceedings. Once again, Andrews defiantly repeated his defence of his colleagues and insisted that he must be free to appoint his own ministers. Over the next three and a half hours, most of those present spoke, with roughly half in favour of change. At least two compromise proposals were aired — that Andrews and Brooke form a new joint government or that Brooke replace Andrews after the estimates. Both were rejected. No formal vote was taken but it was far from certain that the Prime Minister enjoyed the support of a majority of those present. It was evident that, if he continued as leader, six ministers would leave the government

(Basil Brooke, Brian Maginess, Maynard Sinclair, Dehra Parker, John MacDermott and William Lowry) and that the party in parliament and beyond would be irretrievably divided. Clearly shocked and saddened, he reluctantly decided to resign and accordingly next day reported to the governor. Before the meeting dispersed, a resolution was proposed: 'that the party should go forward unitedly and that any disagreement that had been shown should be healed up now'.[82] No vote is recorded.

Andrews' unwillingness to make the cabinet changes urged upon him stemmed in part from loyalty to long-serving colleagues, some of whom had enjoyed the confidence of Craig and, in some cases, even Carson. The *Belfast News Letter* stated that he had 'sacrificed himself on the altar of loyalty'.[83] His obduracy was reinforced, however, not only by the context of war but also his own political weakness. He publicly claimed that the members of the cabinet 'were the best available',[84] whilst privately he recognised and was concerned about their inadequacies. Spender referred to his 'fear ... to make cabinet changes'. Some of his ministers made his position no easier by indicating their determination to remain in office (one stated that he did 'not intend to retire except by the hand of God').[85] His uncharacteristic inflexibility also owed something to the confrontational manner in which the unionist backbenchers had raised the issue of government restructuring — their secret meeting, their list of named ministers to be dismissed (including Andrews) and, the unkindest cut, their leaking of the entire proceedings to the press. In any case he regarded cabinet appointments as being the prerogative of the Prime Minister, to be accepted by others as a *fait accompli*.

Brooke dismissed contemporary allegations that he had conspired against Andrews' leadership. He had entirely failed to anticipate either the timing or the scale of the party revolt in January 1943. This was partly because of his absorption in departmental matters, and also his keen interests outside politics. His role during the crucial weeks which followed was a passive one: he made no attempt to contact or instruct disaffected unionist backbenchers and those junior ministers who sought his advice did so of their own volition. The talent of the dissidents lessens the credibility of any claim that they were used to engineer his rise. In his diary, he expressed doubts as to the desirability of becoming premier and uneasiness about his own suitability for the position. He wrote: 'No-one with any ambition would do it'. He continued: 'I might be alright as departmental chief but I don't know that I would have the political acumen to make a good prime minister'.[86] The final outcome was not the product of his manipulative skills or unsated appetite for power. Rather, the Andrews government collapsed under the accumulated weight of its own incompetence. It had proved incapable of responding adequately to the demands of war.

4
FROM THE ASHES, A NEW BEGINNING
1943-45

Brooke as Prime Minister

Brooke was an Anglo-Irish landlord from Co. Fermanagh who, in due course, became the province's longest serving Prime Minister (he resigned on 24 March 1963). In 1943, he already was a highly divisive figure: he had made a series of intemperate speeches ten years earlier, in which he had appealed to 'loyalists ... wherever possible to employ Protestant lads and lassies'.[1] Nonetheless he had much to offer the Unionist Party. By Stormont standards he was young (54 years of age) and had a considerable breadth of experience. After attending school in Pau in the south of France, and Winchester, he had proceeded to the military academy at Sandhurst. As he later explained, 'no great thought had been put into the idea of career', but soldiering seemed 'the most obvious'.[2] Subsequently he saw service with the 10th Hussars in India, South Africa and on the western front (1914-18) and in the Dardanelles. He won the Military Cross and the *Croix de Guerre*, was mentioned in dispatches, rose to the rank of captain and became *aide-de-camp* to Major-General Julian Bing.

Soon after returning to his estates at Colebrooke, ('the great love'[3] of his life) Brooke had helped initiate, organize and head the special constabulary in his native county during 1920-22. This proved to be the natural stepping-stone to a political career. In 1929, he entered the Northern Ireland parliament and rose rapidly, becoming an able, energetic and uniquely effective cabinet member, a fact recognised and commented on by a number of leading British ministers and officials. As Minister of Agriculture, 1933-40, he played a central role in boosting Northern Ireland's food output and, at Commerce (1941-43), he helped substantially to improve the productivity of the major munitions firms and to reduce unemployment. He had a genial, affable personality; MacDermott described him as 'on easy terms with all men'.[4] He had also much valued contacts in Britain: Alan Brooke was his uncle and the Duke of Gloucester, King George VI's brother, honeymooned at Colebrooke. From the beginning of the conflict, he had radiated a genuine sense of war urgency, rooted in his military background. Twenty-seven members of his extended family served in World War II, including his three sons: two of them lost their lives. At the height of the recent political crisis, on 26 March 1943, he recorded in his diary: 'It is a sad day; the War Office reported that Julian [his eldest son] has been killed in action'.[5]

In 1944, Tom Harrisson described Brooke as 'diplomatic, intelligent, lively ... considered by some of his party too advanced and too liberal. There have been considerable moves to replace him'.[6] Certainly as premier, Brooke displayed more courage and energy than either Andrews or Craigavon in his later years. Arguably, however, he ultimately lacked vision and failed to rise to that higher level of leadership which does not simply pander to supporters but dares to chip away at their prejudices. His ministers were little known but, by Stormont standards, were young and progressive . Four, including Brooke himself, had served in the previous government; the remaining three had never held government office. Most were competent, and had proven administrative ability. From the outset, Spender believed that they would 'carry out [their] duties very effectively.'[7] Probably all of them had been convinced for some time of the need for a change of leadership. Harry Midgley, of the Commonwealth Labour Party, was the only non-Unionist to reach cabinet rank between 1921-71. It seems likely that he would have refused to join a reconstructed government led by Andrews but he happily became Minister of Public Security, despite NILP jibes that he was a 'quisling'.[8] The *Belfast Telegraph* described his inclusion as 'timely recognition of a man who has the courage of his principles'.[9]

In appointing him, Brooke's intention was not only to take advantage of the best talent available and to broaden his government's representation within Northern Ireland; he also wished to make a favourable impression at Westminster. Officials there had long been advocating that the Stormont administration should be composed on a more representative basis. Brooke appointed no deputy and, applying the lessons of recent experience, advised cabinet members at their first meeting not to regard their positions as permanent. They then also 'unitedly resolved to maintain the existing constitutional position, to bring greater drive and energy into Northern Ireland's war effort and to advance as far as possible the government's preparations for dealing with the problems of the post-war period'.[10]

Party Unity – A Priority

In attempting to achieve the first of these, the Prime Minister regarded it as vital from the outset to restore and preserve Unionist Party unity. It became an obsession and an undoubted source of weakness. In 1943, however, it was an urgent consideration because of the bitterness and hostility which had resulted from Andrews' fall. The change of government and, more particularly, the manner in which it had occurred, caused deep and enduring tensions throughout the movement. There was considerable residual sympathy felt for the 'old guard' in the influential but increasingly unrepresentative committees of the Ulster Unionist Council and within sections of the unionist press, notably the *Belfast News Letter* and the *Northern Whig*. Most of the ex-ministers felt embittered by recent events. Some undoubtedly shared the late premier's conviction that they had been manipulated from office by backstairs intrigue.

Moreover, Andrews was disappointed by his own exclusion from Brooke's cabinet; there was a recent precedent — Chamberlain, though dying from cancer, had been included in Churchill's new administration, in May 1940. Though he devoted more energy to the family business and became more active in the Orange Order, he also attended the Commons regularly until his retirement in 1953. As a backbencher, he was acutely sensitive to any perceived criticism of his government. He invariably attacked, with Glentoran's support, less popular aspects of Brooke's policy and, on occasion, even briefed disaffected MPs on points of criticism which they might raise in debate. He persisted with his claim that when in office he had reached an understanding with the imperial chancellor, enabling him to do almost anything he wished, despite the context of war. In making this unjustified assertion, he tended by implication to belittle the achievements of his successor. In early March 1944, his querulous behaviour attracted a strongly-worded but ineffective rebuke from Lord Londonderry. In an open letter to Andrews, the marquess described the office of Prime Minister of Northern Ireland as 'one of the most difficult and arduous amongst the positions of honour and duty in the British Empire'. After referring to Brooke's 'wisdom and tireless energy' he continued, 'in all criticisms ... we should carefully consider how far they affect for good or evil the unity of purpose and action on which not only the winning of the war but all we are fighting for depends'.[11]

Overall, Brooke responded to his political and personal problems with courage, ability and confidence. He had anticipated strong initial opposition to his cabinet, given the nature of events in early 1943. But, in any case, throughout his premiership, he was convinced that the Unionist Party could well disintegrate at any time due to the contrasting class background of its members and their conflicting political beliefs and aspirations. He regarded its unity as, at best, tenuous and ultimately dependent on the 'border question'. Without it, he noted in his diary on 10 October 1943, 'various opinions would make themselves felt'.[12]

On taking office, Brooke therefore tried in a variety of ways to improve the party's cohesion and raise its morale. He invited a succession of leading

British politicians — both labour and conservative — to address public meetings in the province, including Stafford Cripps, Herbert Morrison, Hugh Dalton, Oliver Lyttleton and J.J. Llewellin. He considered that his greatest coup, however, was the visit of George VI on 17 July 1945. Unlike Andrews, he also regarded publicity as a top priority. Soon after becoming Prime Minister, he set up a cabinet committee with this specific responsibility and appointed public relations officers in London and Belfast. He himself constantly briefed and sought advice from journalists and at his first cabinet meeting exhorted his colleagues to do the same.

Brooke had earlier advised Andrews that the parliamentary party was the 'only thing that mattered'[13] and, as Prime Minister, he employed a variety of tactics to win over and sustain its support. He sought to improve consultative procedures between ministers and backbenchers on proposed legislation. He held meetings more frequently so that cabinet policy could be explained and defended, alternative measures considered and grievances aired. Not infrequently, he interjected an appeal for party unity, urging its necessity in the interests of both the war effort and the preservation of the union. On occasion, he indicated his own willingness to resign, but stressed that the alternative to his continued leadership was a wartime general election. In addition, he set in motion a process of Unionist Party reorganisation — it had been under active consideration since the final months of the Andrews government. The Conservative Party was the model adopted. The holding of an annual conference and appointment of a paid party chairman were amongst the earliest innovations which resulted.

In March 1944, Brooke proposed that Andrews be re-elected President of the UUC and later helped ensure that Glentoran was appointed as party treasurer and trustee. These carefully modulated and calculated steps reflected the Prime Minister's mounting confidence in his own authority. He noted privately (in July 1944) that he was 'quite prepared' to take them now whereas he was not 'going to appear as an appeaser before'.[14] No doubt partly in reciprocation, Andrews proposed and Glentoran seconded his nomination as party leader at a specially convened standing committee meeting held in March 1945. It was certainly a response which Brooke valued. He later commented that hitherto he had had 'no status'[15] and had become leader merely by virtue of being premier. Nonetheless, for the moment, the presidency eluded him. When eventually Andrews did resign the position in 1947, Glentoran succeeded him (until his death three years later) even though Brooke had indicated his willingness to accept it, if it was offered to him. At the time he reflected despondently on how residual sympathy for the 'old guard' could even still influence unionist voting behaviour.

Political Controversy Unavoidable

Like Craigavon and Andrews, Brooke sought as far as possible to avoid making controversial decisions in wartime, when a general election was impracticable and disunity might disrupt the war effort. Nonetheless as premier he was more active and enterprising than his immediate predecessor. In addition a number of divisive issues arose — some self-imposed, others inherited or related to the war — which required his immediate response. They served to distract him from the priorities which he and his colleagues had agreed at their first cabinet meeting. Amongst them was his decision in February 1944 to ask his recently appointed Minister of Education, Rev. Professor Robert Corkey, to resign. Sir Basil was satisfied that in spite of repeated warnings, his minister had consistently neglected his duties; he had attended his department, then based in Portrush, on just three occasions during the previous six months. He was the first departmental head to be replaced by a Northern Ireland premier for alleged incompetence in the history of the state. Spender, whose advice strongly favoured his ejection,had earlier expressed unease at Brooke's inclusion of two clerics in his government (Rev. R. Moore at Agriculture was the other). This did not imply any Christian zeal on Sir Basil's part — he had lost his religious faith during the first world war. The political significance of Corkey's dismissal was heightened when he (Corkey) insisted in a public statement that it had been precipitated by disagreements on fundamental matters of principle. Specifically he alleged that with regard to the major measure of educational reform then imminent, Brooke was not committed to the compulsory provision of religious instruction in state schools. He also claimed that an anti-presbyterian bias operated in the administration of his own ministry, connived in by Brooke, but attributable mainly to the influence of its permanent secretary and parliamentary secretary.

The effect of Corkey's allegations was to impose a severe additional strain on party loyalty. He received strong sectional support from the members of his own denomination having, in Spender's phrase, introduced a 'sectarian'[16] point of view. Brooke's backbench sympathisers therefore advised him not to seek a commons resolution of confidence in his government, as they anticipated that it would be defeated. Yet the alarm generated by the controversy regarding future educational policy would appear to have been without foundation. When the cabinet first discussed the question fully, three months later, the principle of compulsory religious instruction was unanimously and unhesitantly endorsed by all. The far-reaching nature of the legislation did of course raise a number of sensitive and complex issues, such as the level of public funding for catholic schools and questions arising out of the teaching of religious education in the state sector. That these required three more years to resolve was due in part to the bitterness aroused within the Unionist Party by Corkey's dismissal.

From its inception, the government's attention was distracted by another similarly delicate matter, which had for several years been a source of tension within the unionist movement. Ministers experienced persistent pressure from local councillors, high-ranking party officials and some local associations to restore immediately to the formerly discredited Belfast Corporation those powers transferred to administrators in 1942. They were sympathetic in their response, anxious to remove a long-standing source of contention and of grievance, but also concerned to prevent a recurrence of the corruption and nepotism which had previously disfigured the administration of the borough. In 1943, they agreed therefore to a measure which returned some functions to the council but restricted its powers of patronage and conferred exclusive authority to place contracts in the hands of the town clerk and town solicitor. But this proposal was so severely criticised by dissatisfied councillors, who in Spender's view, had learnt nothing from past experience, that the cabinet decided to abandon all legislation on the question until it had passed out of controversy. Eventually one year later, a bill which retained the earlier conditions relating to contracts was sponsored by the government. Though it had received almost unanimous support at a preliminary meeting of Unionist MPs, a vociferous minority ferociously and unexpectedly attacked it during the second reading debate. Once more Brooke decided not to proceed and, suspecting a conspiracy amongst his backbench 'revolters' (i.e. critics), made immediate changes in the composition of the Whip's office.

The issue was finally resolved when, in the spring of 1945, the government relented and introduced legislation which in essence restored to the Corporation its original functions. It passed through the Commons quickly with little debate and without controversy. There was by then a widespread feeling that the council had been sufficiently punished for past, almost forgotten, misdeeds. The three and a half-year suspension period originally imposed was nearing completion whilst the restrictions proposed earlier by the cabinet had been consistently denigrated as undemocratic and therefore unacceptable. Government members themselves hoped that their action would help soothe internal party divisions, particularly at a time when they were already conducting complex negotiations over future electricity and transport provision. It was in Brooke's view 'politically quite wrong that the representatives of one third of the population should be antagonistic.'[17]

For some time, however, the most widespread and persistent criticism of the government had centred on the province's acute housing shortage. By 1943, ministers were convinced that this had become the major focus of current public concern, surpassing unemployment. They concluded that even in wartime it was politically necessary to do something. The roots of the problem predated the outbreak of war. Northern Ireland officials recognised that during the inter-war years, local provision had been allowed to lag significantly behind other United Kingdom regions. Stormont government housing subsidies and the overall house construction rate were then at best half the British level, and no scheme of slum clearance was attempted (four million houses were built in Britain between the wars; only 50,000 in the six counties). The situation would have been worse, had relative demand not been lower in the province as a result of low population growth, low marriage rates and low levels of internal migration.

The housing problem had of course become more acute in wartime owing principally to bomb damage and also to the lack of new building and inadequate maintenance. Ironically the population of Northern Ireland was then reaching its peak growth rate since the Famine. During the Belfast blitz, 56,600 houses had been damaged; of these 3,200 had been totally demolished and 4,000 reduced to a state of acute disrepair. As a consequence, 15,000 Belfast citizens had no homes and 100,000 had been left temporarily homeless whilst repairs were carried out. The Rev. J. Woodburn (ex-Presbyterian Moderator) after going 'around some of the devastated areas' felt constrained to approach John MacDermott. He wrote: 'I hope and trust that they [the houses] will never be rebuilt again... A minister said to me, whose congregation had been bombed... if he could get the people entirely out of the way he would be happy if Hitler would come and bomb the place flat.'[18] In December 1941 a Belfast Corporation survey stated that in 'bad' working class areas people were living in 'mere hovels...[in] indescribable filth and squalor'.[19]

Northern Ireland's first official housing enquiry was initiated by Brooke soon after becoming premier and reported in 1944; for the first time the scale of the problem was authoritatively quantified. It estimated that 60% of Belfast citizens were living in poorer areas with at least 60 houses per acre, and that 37% inhabited overcrowded or unfit dwellings. It was calculated that 23,500 new houses were urgently required for the city alone and 100,000 for the six counties overall. On 10 August 1944, William Grant, then Minister of Health, informed his colleagues that there were over 43,000 'totally unfit houses'[20] in the province. Nonetheless, the obstacles blocking an effective cabinet response proved insurmountable until well after the war. These included the customary dilatoriness of local authorities in fulfilling their housing obligations, due to conservatism, inertia and financial constraints. In a number of instances, political difficulties also arose; councillors were concerned that the provision of new permanent homes might upset the delicate sectarian balance in electoral areas, so enabling their opponents to gain control of the council. In addition construction was impeded by wartime shortages of building materials and labour. These problems were compounded by avoidable confusion over the precise division of responsibility between the ministries of Finance and Home Affairs and between central and local government. Finally, even if these matters had been resolved, there remained the further complication of attracting treasury approval and funding for schemes; at the time house building in Britain had been virtually abandoned owing to the more urgent priorities of war.

Nonetheless, in late 1943, the Stormont government made representations to London appealing for financial support for a regional housing programme. When Westminster agreed, with reluctance, to underwrite the construction of 250 houses within six months, William Lowry (Home Affairs) greeted the proposal with scorn. 'The people', he suggested 'would reply that they had asked for bread and been offered a stone'.[21] In November 1943, the Treasury agreed to 750 being constructed. But Belfast Corporation responded by claiming that no suitable sites for their construction were available within the city boundary. Later (in November 1944) it indicated its intention to take no further action until building costs had fallen.

In order to expedite progress in the city and elsewhere the cabinet had already decided (in July 1944) to establish a Housing Trust. It was a radical initiative, adopted by despairing ministers faced with an acute problem aggravated by war. It accepted and applied the principle of nationalisation; it was a corporate body, empowered to secure in coordination with local authorities the provision of housing accommodation for workers and to allocate it strictly on the basis of need. The associated legislation (the Housing Bill) elicited a predictably hostile response from unionist backbenchers, some of them ex-ministers, and from high ranking civil servants such as Spender. They claimed that such centralisation was unprecedented and unwarranted, and expressed concern regarding the respective roles of private enterprise and local government in meeting future peacetime housing needs. Dr William Lyle attributed the measure to the sinister socialist influence being exercised within the government by Harry Midgley (Minister of Labour). He said of him 'some of his views are abhorrent to me, especially this one of nationalisation. I hope as he grows older, more mellow, more mature, and gets rather more common sense than he has at present, he will drop these obnoxious views'.[22] Midgley was 52 years of age at the time.

The Housing Trust came to be regarded as a considerable success. The initiative illustrates Brooke's essential pragmatism and his keen awareness of the changing mood and expectations of the electorate. He was anxious to respond to those popular pressures which had earlier helped precipitate his predecessor's fall. He regarded the restoration and preservation of party unity not as a mere distraction, but as the vital key to fulfilling his government's first agreed priority 'to maintain the existing constitutional position'. This apart, he and his colleagues devoted their efforts to achieving the others — bringing 'greater drive and energy' to the province's war effort and advancing as far as possible 'preparations for dealing with the problems of the post war period'.[23]

Post War Planning

Because of his concern that he might otherwise arouse unrealisable expectations, Andrews had at first reacted cautiously to the Beveridge report. He observed in December 1942 that it was 'a lengthy document' and it was therefore 'not possible...to express an opinion' but he continued 'if an act is passed in Great Britain to give effect to ... [the Beveridge proposals],... . His Majesty's government here will certainly ask parliament to agree to a similar measure'.[24]

Brooke likewise had doubts about the practicality of the report when first published. But when Prime Minister, he and his colleagues declared their intention to follow Westminster in implementing its recommendations and almost immediately set in motion the first practical steps. They initiated the first ever public enquiry to quantify how far the six counties lagged behind Great Britain, not just in its housing programme but in its health and education services. Parallel investigations were conducted into local transport facilities and planning.

The substantial expansion of governmental responsibility envisaged by the cabinet contributed also to the first major reallocation of functions between the various Northern Ireland departments since 1921. This issue had first been considered during the spring of 1943. It had arisen then partly because of the foreseeable closure of the Ministry of Public Security — its functions were directly related to the war and the justification for its retention was steadily diminishing. Moreover, for some time pressure had been mounting for the formation of a Ministry of Health. Also there was a widespread perception that the duties of the Ministry of Home Affairs were too disparate and unwieldy to be conducive to administrative efficiency (they included local government, law and order, transport etc). In September 1943, Sir Francis Floud, a British civil servant, investigated the workings of the Stormont government and produced recommendations. In due course it was agreed to create a new Ministry of Health and Local Government and to merge the Ministries of Home Affairs and Public Security.

Implementation in 1944-5 was complicated by the political context. Ministers were reluctant to relinquish functions which they had only recently acquired, fearing that the electorate would conclude that they were 'unable to cope with'[25] the work done by their predecessors. Also during the consequent cabinet reshuffle, unionist backbenchers blocked the Prime Minister's choice of Midgley as Minister of Heath. They considered that as a non-Unionist and a professed socialist he might 'do harm there',[26] at a time when major national health service legislation was imminent. Brooke was obliged therefore to retract the appointment. But, intent on preserving the government's 'coalition' appearance, he eventually persuaded his reluctant minister to accept the Ministry of Labour portfolio instead. The new ministry was allocated to William Grant.

The economy represented the government's other major area of attempted post-war planning. As at Westminster, Stormont ministers were committed to a policy aimed at full employment when hostilities ended. After mid-1944, however, their feelings of apprehension about future prospects soared. The flow of munitions contracts, which had always been volatile as well as variable in content, began to dry up. As a result, the major industrial firms began to lay off substantial numbers, particularly of their male labour force. The cabinet was concerned that when hostilities ended, unemployment would rapidly reach 1930s levels; it had already doubled between September-December 1944 (from c.10,000 to c.20,000 insured workers) and was rising. When the Ministry of Labour estimated the likely cost of applying the Beveridge report to the province it assumed an unemployment rate of 12.5%, some 4% higher than the projection for Great Britain. In February 1945, Maynard Sinclair, the Minister of Finance, suggested to his colleagues that no Northern Ireland government could possibly survive in office, if during the post-war years the percentage of jobless locally remained 'substantially above'[27] that of other regions in the United Kingdom.

Certainly from an early stage in the conflict, there is evidence of popular unease and fatalism about employment prospects when it ended. By October 1941 male unemployment had dropped to 5% and the government regarded one third of this hard-core as unemployable — on health grounds or because of poor industrial records or suspected IRA membership. Moya Woodside recorded a conversation with her maid at the time. She wrote

> her [the maid's] father works as a riveter in the shipyard. This morning she said 'father's earning good money now but he's saving like mad to have something left when the war is over and he'll be out of work again'. She added that 'most of his workmates are drinking all their extra pay.'[28]

Brooke fully shared these anxieties though not the fatalism and as premier expended much of his energy in attempting to devise solutions. Thus, in September 1943, a post-war reconstruction committee was formed — its purpose to anticipate and formulate responses to the province's post-war problems. Six months later a government minister, Sir Roland Nugent, was given overall responsibility for the development and coordination of planning. Meanwhile legislation was prepared at Stormont, based on measures taken before the war and concerned to induce new industry to locate in the province in peacetime. Both the unionist leadership and local business interests regarded the dismantling of the wartime economic controls imposed by Westminster (on capital investment, raw materials and labour, and also the rationing of consumer goods) as a peacetime priority. Meanwhile Brooke and his colleagues constantly pressed imperial departments for further orders, attempted to clarify more precisely with them their respective areas of governmental responsibility in generating employment in the six counties and sought better liaison with British ministers regarding their post-war plans and any future legislation which might affect the region. They were especially anxious that Northern Ireland should be officially designated a 'development area' by the British Board of Trade, so entitling it to special consideration after the war and (they hoped) helping to eradicate unemployment.

Brooke's commitment to the Beveridge report and to parity of social services with Britain and his apprehension at the approaching spectre of severe recession when the war ended, all contributed to his continuing enthusiasm for the introduction of conscription. In early 1945 he became aware of Westminster's intention to retain compulsory military service (i.e. to introduce national service) after hostilities had ended, and he immediately urged that it be applied to the province as well. This appealed to him partly on political grounds — its introduction would underline the region's constitutional status within the union. Above all in pleading his case, he was aware of the likely economic benefits. It would, for example, in itself lower unemployment levels, by mopping up surplus labour and therefore ease the difficulties of reinstating in civilian life those who had been demobilised. Crucially, Brooke hoped that by thus 'accepting the obligations of common citizenship' it would enable Britain to treat the six counties more generously. He anticipated that imperial ministers might do so by contributing more liberally to the mounting costs of Northern Ireland's social services, facilitating its efforts to achieve full employment and designating the region a 'development area' after the war. Conversely, Sir Basil feared that if conscription was not applied it would cause 'ill feeling' elsewhere in the United Kingdom and so make it 'difficult for Britain to help'.[29] He had noted, when Minister of Commerce, that the continuation of voluntary recruitment in Ulster was 'so often used by the imperial authorities in production questions'[30] to justify their reluctance to allocate contacts there. In making his request, he anticipated that the war cabinet might well respond as before by saying it would be 'more trouble than it was worth'.[31] He therefore stressed that after the war, larger numbers would be available for military service than before (in 1941), and that any disruption which might result from its application would have much less grave consequences in peacetime. Such was his enthusiasm for this policy that he even favoured making a discreet approach to the catholic bishops to establish whether more generous public funding of church schools would lessen their traditional opposition to its introduction. He suggested to his cabinet colleagues that initial contact should be made with minority 'leaders'[32] — presumably nationalist politicians. No more formal lines of communication appeared to have existed between the government and the catholic community.

When the conscription issue was raised in 1941, Moya Woodside had noted the mood of cynicism locally. She wrote 'feelings seem to be that Stormont is clutching at this as a way out of the unemployment problem, to be solved at England's expense'.[33] British ministers and officials had then been divided on the issue, but in 1945 they unanimously rejected Brooke's request outright. In their view his well rehearsed and wide-ranging arguments amounted to 'no case at all'.[34] They considered that it would be quite 'indefensible'[35] for Westminster to introduce conscription into Northern Ireland for economic reasons and that to apply it after hostilities had ended would be to invite universal condemnation. In 1941, military necessity had enhanced its legitimacy. Likewise, they believed that Brooke and his colleagues would themselves be exposed to ridicule and opprobrium if they were to introduce military service at a time when it involved no risk to the conscripts. One further vital consideration helped determine their response: the sincerely-held conviction that Brooke's request was not in the best interests of Ulster or the preservation of the union. Clearly influenced by the experience of war, the British establishment had come to value the latter more highly. Thus, Charles Markbreiter (assistant secretary at the Home Office with responsibility for the province) observed on 9 May 1945 — the day following VE day — 'the important thing is that the affairs of Northern Ireland be so conducted that the unionist ascendancy be maintained. Nothing should be done to provoke rebellion.... by a large minority who can always look for support from across the border'.[36] On 12 November 1946, Attlee informed Westminster that the National Service Act would apply 'to Great Britain only'.

5

'HALF AT WAR?'
NORTHERN IRELAND'S WARTIME ROLE
1939-1945

Northern Ireland's Wartime Performance:
Economic Output and Role

Charles Markbreiter's comments reflect the fact that, irrespective of the decisions taken regarding conscription, relations between the two United Kingdom governments had become warmer and closer by 1945 than probably at any time in the past. From a Northern Ireland perspective this was almost certainly the most significant outcome of the conflict. Arguably it was not primarily related to any outstanding commitment shown or sacrifice made in wartime by the parliament or people of Northern Ireland. Its major munitions firms had performed poorly, at least until 1942. In the absence of compulsory military service, the level of voluntary recruitment was a constant source of disappointment, even embarrassment, to local ministers. Nor did the unionist leadership itself set an example of sacrifice. When Britain had faced defeat in 1940 and Craig had been invited to enter into discussions with de Valera, he had without compunction placed the narrow interests of the six counties and the preservation of the union above loyalty to crown and empire and the crushing of fascism. The Andrews' government's mishandling of the conscription question, industrial relations and post-war reconstruction had likewise helped generate strains between Stormont and Westminster.

Nevertheless after an uncertain beginning, Northern Ireland's material contributions to the war effort and, crucially, its strategic significance for the allied cause increased beyond all earlier recognition. That it should have attracted the attention of the Luftwaffe was entirely predictable as well as tragic. When just after the Easter Sunday raid Eduard Hempel, the German Minister, came by appointment to see J.P. Walshe, Minister of External Affairs in Dublin, he sought to justify the attack. Walshe recorded their conversation at the time, and saying to him that

> it was a pity that the German government had departed from its policy of leaving the six county area alone. I was afraid that the casualties were very

heavy and that the bombing had been indiscriminate. Dr Hempel replied that he felt quite sure that his government would not have ordered a raid on Belfast if it had not become absolutely essential for the prosecution of the war. Belfast had become a very important port, especially for the trans-shipment of foodstuffs and to abstain any longer from bombing the port and the industrial area around it, would have greatly handicapped the German blockade of Great Britain.[1]

Likewise at the time the German media projected Belfast as a vital industrial base and trading centre, one of the 'main channels through which foodstuffs and war materials had entered Britain.'[2] Robert Fisk writes that the wartime 'achievements of the six counties...involved real efforts and sacrifices.'[3]

Soon after VE Day, Brooke expressed the private conviction that the north's cumulative output of food and munitions since 1939 had been 'staggering'.[4] He was particularly proud of the achievements of its farmers: partly due to his personal role as minister, their performance had been impressive from

Stirlings and Sunderlands, both synonymous with Short and Harlands, at Queen's Island, January 1944; the strategically vulnerable Harbour Power Station is in the background
Public Record Office of Northern Ireland

the outset. By 1945 they had almost doubled their total acreage under the plough (flax acreage alone rose six-fold) and had provided Britain with an average of £3 million worth of cattle and sheep per year at current values and also 20% of its supplies of home produced eggs (300 million in 1944 alone). In four of the six wartime winters, 25,000 gallons of liquid milk were despatched daily to Scotland from Ulster ports. Overall, though productivity was poor and the structure of agriculture distorted during the war (even Brooke later conceded that tillage expansion was 'overdone'[5]), local farm income rose more than in Great Britain, wages rose faster and income per head caught up partially with the levels found in rural areas elsewhere in the United Kingdom. By 1945 Northern Ireland's official war history claimed that 'to go south was to be transported in a matter of minutes from the 20th to the 17th century'. It added that 'within five years, Ulster farming had been substantially mechanised.'[6]

For Northern Ireland industry the war also disrupted and transformed pre-war trends. During the inter-war period, output had declined both in volume and value. The Belfast shipyards failed to recover from the severe drop in tonnage launched that was evident in the years 1920-24; simultaneously, linen manufacture suffered from a sustained contraction in export sales. The long-term collapse in demand for these two pillars of the local economy was not offset by the increased production of relatively small firms in, for example, the tobacco, engineering, building, food and drink sectors. After 1939 however, the old staple industries of the north-east experienced a new lease of life. Net industrial production in the six counties rose by almost two thirds between 1935-49 (compared with less than 40% in Great Britain); the size of the local manufacturing labour force expanded by roughly 50% and output per worker increased by more than 10%. A measurable gap in living standards between north and south of the border began to emerge, which widened steadily until the 1960s.

By 1942, as Northern Ireland moved nearer to achieving full employment, Brooke felt justified in declaring that the region was 'pulling her weight... and had we been able to start as soon as England we should have very little to complain of'.[7] On 24 July 1945, he presented the House with a review of the province's economic contribution over the course of the conflict. His air of satisfaction was at least partially justified. He began his section on industry with shipbuilding — though his relationship with the management of Harland and Wolff had at no time been better than hostile. Between 1940-44, Belfast's shipyards had produced 140 warships including six aircraft carriers, three cruisers, two large depot ships, and a host of corvettes, minesweepers and frigates. In addition, 123 merchant ships had been launched (10% of the total output of the United Kingdom) and 3,000 ships had been repaired or converted (up to 100 at any one time). The company had also diversified its production, which included 500 tanks, numerous gun-mountings and ordnance pieces and over 13 million aircraft parts. In 1932, it had experienced 'virtual closure';[8] in 1944 its labour force peaked at 35,800. Its long term prospects seemed bright, given that both Germany and Japan had been 'neutralised as competitors' as a result of the war. In addition Harland and Wolff managed the Foyle yard in Londonderry which was re-opened by the Admiralty in 1940 (it had previously been operated by the North Ireland Shipbuilding Company between 1912 and 1924). It now acted as a repair and service base for Atlantic convoy escorts; its dry dock was lengthened, new fitters and repair shops were opened and it remained in service until its demolition in 1946. Shipbuilding also revived at Warrenpoint from 1943; tank landing craft were produced by the Newry firm, Smith and Pearson, and some were used in the D Day landings in Normandy.

Meanwhile at the Short and Harland aircraft factory, some of the problems which had earlier afflicted the company had been at least partially overcome. Its reorganisation — it was taken over by the government in March 1943 — contributed to a marked improvement in its performance. As a result, a Stormont official estimated that, by February 1944, the total of days lost through bad time keeping had already fallen by as much as 300-400% in some shops. Five weeks later, Stafford Cripps (Minister of Aircraft Production) informed the Commons that the number of aircraft delivered by the firm had shown an increase of 69% during its first twelve months under new management; in the meantime the size of its workforce had actually decreased. (It had been formed in 1936 and had given employment to 560 by 1937, and 11,319 by 1941). Cumulatively, its wartime output had not been unimpressive. It had completed 1,200 Stirling bombers and 125 Sunderland flying boats, sufficient for over 100 squadrons, and carried out repairs to roughly 3,000 heavy, medium and light aircraft. Management problems related to production had been aggravated by the fact that the work was carried out not only at Sydenham but at eleven dispersal factories scattered throughout counties Antrim and Down; these had been hurriedly improvised after the blitz. Meanwhile, numerous other smaller firms had also contributed to supply department contracts. Collectively, the munitions producers in the Belfast area manufactured 75 million shells, 180 million incendiary bullets, 50,000 bayonets and a variety of fittings ranging from submarine valves to components for the Mulberry floating dock used during the Normandy invasion. One third of the ropes required by the War Office were made at Belfast Ropeworks; it produced in total a quarter of a million tons of rope and in addition 50,000 camouflage and cargo nets.

The local textile and clothing industry had greater difficulty in adjusting to war conditions. Output was restricted both by raw material shortages and the disruption of exports which forced some firms to close or to operate only on a part-time basis. Nonetheless, the province's looms wove a total of 200 million yards of cloth for the forces. Hundreds of thousands of servicemen's uniforms were produced in Northern Ireland and 90% of their shirt requirements — 30 million in total, including the bush shirts worn in the North Africa campaign and the demobilisation shirts issued in 1945. Linen firms also diversified production to include parachute webbing and harnesses (2 million flax-fabric parachutes were manufactured in the province during the war years). A significant feature of all local industry in wartime, not just linen and clothing firms but aircraft production, rope making and engineering, was the expansion of female employment. The total number of female insured workers in the six counties increased from 111,900 in 1939 to a peak of 118,600 in 1943.

Members of the Royal Ulster Rifles (2nd Battalion) at La Brèche d'Hermanville, Normandy, around noon, D-Day, 6 June 1944
David Ashe, Langford Lodge Wartime Centre

Despite the palpable contrast in atmosphere between Northern Ireland and Britain observed by Harrisson, outside the factory gates there is evidence of working people contributing individually in support of the war effort with characteristic generosity. When in mid-1940, the *Belfast Telegraph* launched a Spitfire Fund (on 12 August 1940) on lines similar to schemes operating in Britain, its target was '£5,000 for one plane'. By the end of the year £51,000 had been raised, donations coming from all over the six counties; the final total reached by 1945 was £88,633 — enough to purchase 17 aircraft. When the scheme was first announced, the stated intention was 'to enable the humblest in the country the opportunity to share in a project which would make spontaneous appeal to the patriotic instincts of the community'.[9] Moya Woodside's comments would suggest that the 'humblest' did in fact contribute most and that social class largely determined individual responsiveness. She wrote with the cynicism which typified her perception of the media:

> The Spitfire Fund stunt has certainly caught the imagination and astonishing sums are subscribed from working class streets and country towns. It is noticeable that the response from middle and upper class districts is meagre in comparison — presumably because the residents feel that they are already having enough taken off them in rates and taxes. This last fortnight we have been polluted with children coming to the door with collecting sheets.[10]

This reaction may have been fairly representative of her social *milieu*.

The Military Contribution

With regard to Northern Ireland's direct contribution to the allied war effort, even the official war history states voluntary recruitment was 'relatively low'[11] for much of the conflict and comments on the comparative failure of the local recruitment campaign. Nonetheless, even here the province's role was not inconsiderable. There was a powerful tradition within the Anglo-Irish landlord class of service in Britain's armed forces stretching back to Gough and Wellington. David Fraser, Alan Brooke's biographer, writes that the Ulster Plantation 'provided the army with many of its most illustrious names...the roll call echoes down the last two centuries like the music of some noble ceremonial march... Military service came as naturally to them as breathing.' By way of explanation, he states 'Life in Ireland could never be placid or predictable. These families came to identify themselves closely with the country of their adoption...but ancient bitterness survived, feeding on every misfortune, every iniquity...Danger and instability were never far below the surface of elegance, amusement and affection.... Such an atmosphere breeds fighting men.'[12] The list of British army officers of Ulster (nine-county) extraction includes, apart from Brooke himself, Alexander, Auchinleck, Dill, Montgomery and Templer. Individuals from the province rose to prominence in each of the services — for example, W.P. MacArthur became Director General of Army Medical Services; Rear-Admiral W.P. Patterson received the Order of the Bath for his part in the action against the *Bismarck*. Outstanding individual achievements are exemplified in the careers of Col. Robert Blair Mayne of the Special Air Service who, in raids behind enemy lines, destroyed more enemy aircraft — 47 in one day alone — and won more decorations than any other serviceman, and Squadron Leader James Malley who flew more 'ops' (127) than any other RAF pilot.

In total over 38,000 men and women from the six counties are known to have enlisted during World War II. In the opening phase of hostilities 1939-40, local recruits saw action in Norway, north-eastern France and the Low Countries. Later as the conflict spread and the allies seized the offensive, they served as members of eighteen fighting units associated with the province, in every theatre of war — Burma, North Africa, Sicily, Southern Italy, from 'Kent to Cawnpore and from Anzio to Chittagong'.[13] The final stages of the war brought them close to where it had begun — with the Normandy landings, the advance to the Rhineland and the final push from the Rhine to the ancient and inflammable German city of Lübeck.

Belsen, the German concentration camp, shortly after being liberated by the 2nd Army, April 1945
Belfast Telegraph

The memory of some of their experiences has never dimmed. James Molyneaux was one of those who volunteered. He had been motivated to join the RAF partly as a result of the Belfast blitz; he could hear the raids from his home near Aldergrove airport and later saw for himself the devastation caused to the city. Now, in Germany four years later, he witnessed scenes, the 'most staggering and harrowing' of his life, which made the almost incalculable sacrifices of the allies seem justified. He entered the Nazi concentration camp at Belsen in late April, days after it had been liberated by the 2nd Army. His unit had been instructed, as a matter of urgency, to bring up food, medical supplies and blankets. He still vividly recalls the unimaginable suffering there. The camp was clearly visible from a main trunk road that for 700 yards ran ten feet distant from its electrified perimeter fence; the corpses of those who had abandoned hope could be seen, 'their fingers gripped in death'. Inside, 60,000 had been held captive. Huts built to house 30 people were occupied by up to 500. Typhus, typhoid and dysentery were rampant. There was 'not a single able-bodied person among those surviving'. Literally, hundreds were dying daily; bodies littered the compound. He described his 'feeling of disbelief that any human being could do that kind of thing to any other human being.' He felt 'rage' at seeing SS officers who were forced to carry out relief work and dig mass graves 'continuing to ill treat in your presence their victims, who were on the point of death'. He remembers rolls of insulating tape being distributed to British military personnel to enable them to silence the horns of jeeps; the inmates were so weak that 'it was not unknown at the beginning, when drivers sounded...[them]...that they dropped dead with the shock.'[14]

At the time, the allied troops had little awareness that the war was nearly over. On 9 May, the day after the VE day celebrations, Brooke had stated: 'The first great victory has been won, now we must turn with all our skill and all our might to the winning of the second — the victory over Japan.'[15] In fact the war in the east ended much sooner than anticipated; Japan capitulated after H-bomb attacks on Hiroshima and Nagasaki (6 and 9 August 1945). Two weeks earlier, on 31 July, James Magennis, a Catholic, born in October 1919 at 4 Majorca Street in the Donegall Road area of Belfast, had won Ireland's last and Northern Ireland's only Victoria Cross of the war. He had joined the Royal Navy, aged 16, in June 1935, and was finally discharged in October 1949 having served on over a dozen vessels. He received the award for attaching six limpet mines to a Japanese cruiser, the 9,850 ton, 8-inch gun *Takao*, off Borneo. He was transported by midget submarine, XE3. It was a particularly hazardous operation taking him over half an hour. The cruiser was in very clear water so that he was easily visible to those on board throughout, had they looked. Thick barnacles had first to be removed from the ship's sloping bottom, and meanwhile his oxygen supply was leaking bubbles to the surface. At 9.30 pm, the explosion was heard as the charges went up, blowing a hole 30 feet by 60 feet; by then Magennis was 15 miles away. He returned from Singapore to receive his VC from George VI on 11 December 1945. A street was later named after him in the naval township near Gosport and a comic strip made out of his exploits. He had displayed a single-minded devotion to duty and a total disregard for his own safety. After service, he worked in a circus and later as an electrician and a fitter. He settled in Bradford and died in Halifax in February 1986. Five months later his award was auctioned at Sotheby's; it was the first naval Victoria Cross to be sold.[16]

Members of the Royal Air Force and Women's Auxiliary Air Force from the province also served in all theatres and many distinguished themselves

James Magennis attending a civic reception at the City Hall, Belfast, given by the Lord Mayor, Sir Crawford McCullagh, 14 December 1945
Belfast Telegraph

— 14 received Distinguished Service Orders, 240 Distinguished Flying Crosses and 81 Distinguished Flying Medals. The final known casualty figures for men born in Northern Ireland who served in the armed forces and merchant navy in World War II exceeded 4,700. This total includes 2,256 army personnel, 1,112 RAF, 843 Royal Navy and 524 Merchant Navy (figures for women and nursing services are not available). The first RAF fatality was Edmund Sorley, a pilot from south Armagh who was killed on 4 September 1939 during an attack on German ships at Brunsbuttel. With regard to army losses, Ulster's experience in the 1914-18 war, when huge casualty levels were sustained by the 36th (Ulster) Division at the Somme, was not repeated. Rather, throughout 1939-45 the death toll rose gradually; after virtually every major military engagement the names of men from the province appeared in the 'killed in action' columns of local newspapers.[17]

Northern Ireland's Strategic Role

Undoubtedly the cumulative contribution of both men and munitions from the province to the war effort and the shared experience of war, especially the blitz, helped draw both the governments and peoples of Northern Ireland and Great Britain more closely together. It was, however, above all the

R.A.F. Sunderland, Belleek, Co. Fermanagh, returning from the air corridor, over Co. Donegal, west of Lough Erne
Ernie Cromie, Ulster Aviation Society

facts of geography which made Ulster's role in allied victory a much more vital one and which most earned Westminster's gratitude. German conquest and occupation of western Europe, combined with neutral Eire denying Britain access to its harbours and airfields, dramatically enhanced the wartime significance of the province.

The fall of France opened up a new phase in the Battle of the Atlantic by providing Germany with naval and air bases on the ocean's seaboard from which to harass merchant shipping more effectively. Already by December 1939, 220 merchant ships had been sunk by U-boats, prompting a frantic corvette construction programme, to strengthen rapidly the convoy escorts. Many in Britain now came to regret the handing over of the Treaty ports to the Dublin government in 1938. At the time Churchill had opposed it; during debates at Westminster he predicted that the south might well be neutral in a future European conflict and described the bases as 'the sentinel towers of the western approaches' and England's 'life defences'.[18] Later that year in November, de Valera indicated that there was no question of them being returned; 'they are ours', he stated and 'any attempt to bring pressure...can only result in bloodshed.'[19] Twelve months later, in November 1939, when the imperial government requested their use the Taoiseach replied 'persistence means war'.[20] In response, from mid-1940, some British military leaders pressed for the invasion of Ireland. Churchill stated threateningly that there were 'ways to get the ports back';[21] he had commented earlier on 6 November 1940 that it was 'a grievous and heavy burden that we cannot use the south and west coasts of Ireland to refuel our flotillas and aircraft'.[22] This Commons speech set in circulation a further cycle of invasion rumours in Dublin. Meanwhile Westminster had taken one practical and uncontroversial step — the diversion of the Atlantic convoys around the north coast of Ireland.

These circumstances enormously enhanced Northern Ireland's role in keeping the sea lanes open during the Battle of the Atlantic. Her ports, anchorages and airfields became bases for anti-submarine escorts, maritime reconnaissance and coastal command. Professor Blake said of Londonderry that it 'held the key to victory...[as] our most westerly base for repair, the working up and refuelling of destroyers, corvettes and frigates.' By 1943, when the battle 'finally turned our way' he adds, it 'was the most important escort base in the north western approaches'.[23] The airfields used by the RAF coastal command at Nutts Corner, Long Kesh, Aldergrove, Limavady, Ballykelly, Castle Archdale and Killadeas were also an increasingly significant strategic asset in the U-boat war. In 1943, the record year, 18 (21%) of the 84 submarines destroyed by RAFCC were by aircraft based in Northern Ireland; their final two sinkings of the conflict occurred on 29 and 30 April 1945. During the course of the war an estimated 1900 survivors of U-boat attacks on supply vessels in the north Atlantic were rescued and brought to Londonderry. The locally raised No. 502 (Ulster) Squadron participated in the Battle of the Atlantic when based at Limavady (in the course of the war 169 of its members were killed in action). The effectiveness of coastal command was undoubtedly heightened when, in January 1941, de Valera reached an agreement with the British air ministry permitting their use of an air corridor over southern Irish territory, west of Lough Erne.

Hitherto the RAF had been reluctant to fly over Donegal and favoured building bases in the west of Scotland.[24]

In 1943, Herbert Morrison, the Home Secretary, accurately reviewed Northern Ireland's recent role. He observed 'her strategical position alone ensures that her contribution is a crucial one. The unprotected gap in mid-Atlantic, the stretch of ocean which could not be covered by shore-based aircraft from either side would have been far wider if it had not been for the coastal command bases in Northern Ireland, similarly with the surface patrol crafts whose range would have been lessened without the Ulster bases'.[25] Two months earlier (in a letter to Andrews after the fall of his government), Churchill had laid particular emphasis an another aspect of the province's wartime contribution — that of providing a 'safe' conduit for some of the munitions and food flowing into Britain from North America, under the lend-lease scheme. He observed: 'We were alone and had to face single-handed the full fury of the German attacks...seeking to strangle our life by cutting off the entry to our ports.... Only one great channel of entry remained open. That channel remained open because loyal Ulster gave us full use of the North Irish ports and waters.... But for its loyalty...we should have been confronted with slavery and death.'[26]

The fall of France not only threatened United Kingdom commerce, it also increased the likelihood of a German invasion of Ireland, and Britain regarded

Aerial view of Castle Archdale, Co. Fermanagh, 1945
Ernie Cromie
Ulster Aviation Society

the defence of all 32 counties as central to its national security and indeed survival. Once again, the north undoubtedly played a vital role in the counter-measures which it devised by land, sea and air. Ireland could have provided Germany with an invaluable base from which the Nazi leadership might reasonably have hoped to bomb and blockade Great Britain into submission. It could have been used to devastate western ports and industrial centres such as Bristol, Liverpool and Clydeside, cripple the internal railway network and more effectively strangle trans-Atlantic trade; moreover it was a potential launching pad for the invasion of England. In December 1940 Hitler declared that its occupation could 'lead to the end of the war'; however, as Grand Admiral Raeder pointed out, without control of the sea this was an impracticable and quixotic strategy.[27] Also Churchill actually considered that there could be 'various advantages to us' in a German landing in Ireland. He added: 'We should bomb and fight the German airforce under conditions especially favourable to us... We should take Berehaven...[and we]...should have the greater part of the population [of Ireland] on our side for the first time in history'. In his view 'nothing that can happen in Ireland can be immediately decisive'.[28]

During 1940-41 the *Wehrmacht* devised and considered several varying plans for the invasion of Ireland. In mid-1940, Operation Sealion (the planned attack on Britain, postponed in October) included as a deceptive device the landing of five or six divisions on Eire's southern coast. Meanwhile the plan for Irish landings contained in Operation Green (developed in August 1940) may also have had a diversionary function, but its detailed nature and the extent of its distribution within Germany suggests that a genuine assault, again on the south coast, was being seriously contemplated. A direct attack was considered probably for the last time in January 1941 when General Student advocated a night-time airborne descent on Northern Ireland involving 20,000 paratroopers and 12,000 airborne troops. His objective was to secure a base bounded by Divis mountains, Lough Neagh and west Belfast; this was to be facilitated by a subsidiary drop at Lisburn to immobilise this centre of road and rail communications. He argued that his strategy had a much better prospect of success, if directed against Ulster, than against any comparable target area in southern England.[29]

The feasibility of these plans was enhanced by the fact that Eire, especially if left to its own resources, lay virtually undefended and might not have been able to mobilise a united resistance. In May 1940, it had just 13,300 troops, though this had risen to 41,400 by March 1941. As in the north, Axis success in mid-1940 temporarily stimulated voluntary recruitment. Throughout the 'phoney war' its airforce was woefully ill-equipped, whilst its navy was comprised of 6 motor torpedo boats and two patrol vessels.[30] In effect, Ireland depended on Britain and the United States for its defence. In 1939, the first public information pamphlet published by the Irish Department of Defence was hardly reassuring; it advised citizens in the event of invasion to 'learn first aid' and 'keep a stout heart'. One of its remaining four points contained a strict injunction: 'do not cooperate with...the enemy'.[31] However, the plans which the Dublin government itself devised (in May 1940) to resist German invasion assumed that it would coincide with 'an internal rising by the IRA... with...aid from a foreign power'.[32] That organisation's successful raid on the magazine fort in Phoenix Park in December 1939 underlined the threat which it posed. Meanwhile, Irish intelligence (G2) monitored closely and very successfully its limited but nonetheless alarming contacts with the German *Abwehr*.

British Pressure on Eire to Move From Neutrality

The threat of a German invasion of Ireland profoundly alarmed the British government. When the *Wehrmacht* launched its assault on the Low Countries (10 May 1940), British troops based in the six counties (the 53rd Welsh division) were immediately placed on full alert; all mobile columns were 'placed at one hour's notice to move'[33] and no more than 50% of personnel in each unit were permitted to leave camp at any one time. During that month de Valera was approached with a request to allow British forces into southern Ireland in advance of any German attack; he refused, though some opposition members favoured inviting their entry (Richard Mulcahy) and even abandoning neutrality (James Dillon). Subsequently, attempts to form a joint council for the defence of the 32 counties failed. At an Anglo-Irish government meeting for the coordination of defence, de Valera stated that 'because of the neutral attitude of our people...it would be impossible to have anything like staff talks'.[34] The divisional history of the 53rd records 'so strict was Eire's neutrality that little or no prior discussion on the course of action to be adopted took place'.[35]

During June and July 1940, United Kingdom pressure on the Dublin government to move from its neutrality policy reached its peak. Ministers evaluated the efficacy of economic sanctions and an offer of unity was made to de Valera through Malcom MacDonald. Some senior military officers recited with passion powerful strategic arguments in favour of an invasion of Ireland before Germany struck (British intelligence sources indicated that the Nazi high command would launch an assault on 15 July). But there was little support within the war cabinet for such a drastic course of action. Neville Chamberlain, in particular, opposed; when asked by John Dulanty, the Irish High Commissioner in London (on 5 July) whether or not it was being contemplated, he instantly replied 'Good God, haven't we enough trouble already?'.[36] Sir John Maffey, Britain's ambassador in Dublin, held similar views. He advised the Secretary of State for Dominion Affairs, Lord Cranborne (on 23 December 1940), 'every argument points to the exercise of patience...a friendly and reasoned approach will serve us best.'[37] Nonetheless the Dublin government was sufficiently alarmed by the threatening content of Churchill's speeches and the exasperated tone of the English press that it took the precaution of preparing a plan against British invasion; its main proposed line of resistance was to have been along the line of the rivers Boyne and Blackwater,[38] (the IRA were rumoured to have similar plans to prevent British troops moving south).[39]

The Build up of British Troops in Northern Ireland

In these circumstances, Britain's plans for the defence of Ireland against any prospective German invasion were based mainly on the troops it had deployed in the six counties. Until June 1940 these consisted solely of the 53rd division, which had arrived 'in driblets', virtually untrained, between October 1939 and the following April. During May 1940, its primary function changed from internal security to 'action against enemy forces invading Eire' and 'action to repel an enemy invasion of Northern Ireland'.[40] It lacked the resources to fulfil these tasks. Over the next twelve months, substantial reinforcements arrived and were deployed in virtually every part of the province (the 61st and 48th infantry, 71st and 72nd brigades and 5th division). By late spring 1941, their combined strength peaked at four divisions — the number thought necessary and sufficient to meet the needs of any German attack, as well as stiffen internal security in the north. The arrival of the 5th division in March 1941 was also made possible by improved conditions in Britain itself; by then its coastal and other defences had been strengthened, 'the German air assault had almost shot its bolt', and the likelihood of German invasion had greatly diminished. Consequently Eire was regarded as the one 'soft spot' or strategic weakness left anywhere in the British Isles.[41]

Meanwhile during the summer of 1940, when the prospect of a successful German landing in Ireland was at its height, it was decided to establish in the north special land and air commands to control military operations, and troops were deployed according to their specific role in the plans prepared. The 53rd division was designated to act as the spearhead if Eire was attacked; General Huddleston (GOC of British troops in Northern Ireland) set up headquarters at Lisburn on 12 July and the force located along the border in Fermanagh, Antrim and Down. Cork was regarded as the most likely port of entry, given its proximity to north-west France, and the successful defence of Dublin considered to be critical. Despite periodic rumours, no invasion occurred and, apart from training, military activity was mainly confined to 'vigilance and action against the IRA'. Though it conducted only 'infrequent...minor enterprises', guard duties were 'very heavy, as many as 30% in some units being employed in this way'.[42] In November 1941, as a consequence of the improving war situation and troop congestion in the north, the division transferred to the Welsh border counties.

The 61st division had primary responsibility for the static defence of the six counties, including Belfast. Various forms of German attack were prepared for — a seaborne assault from Norway or France and airborne landings from northern France, as well as the possibility of small-scale raiding parties. It was expected that any substantial assault would be directed towards the beaches along the Antrim and Londonderry coasts; it was thought that these would provide easier access for landing craft from Norway or France than the more rocky, mined east coast which faced Great Britain. By the autumn of 1940, the unfamiliar array of defence emplacements — concrete pillars, barbed wire and concealed firing points — amazed those travelling even through parts of rural Ulster. Moya Woodside recorded her impressions when driving to a Co. Antrim village 30 miles from Belfast. She wrote 'the preparations along the road are fantastic... Barriers of concrete and railway sleepers, three and four deep, bar the exit from [the city] and entrances and exits of every village *en route*, usually with pill boxes as well. All the bridges even on small secondary roads are mined and a cross-roads in the heart of the country is fortified as if to hold up an advancing army'.[43] Likewise, Newry was affected physically more than by any war since the seventeenth century. The town was garrisoned, fortifications built, 'suddenly all over the town sprang up massive reinforced gun emplacements ... streets and bridges were semi-blocked by dragon teeth [metal and concrete blockades]'.[44]

In the spring of 1942, the *Wehrmacht* appeared all but invincible. Germany's domination of Europe was almost complete; its forces had occupied Paris for two years and stood poised before Moscow; its allies, Italy and Japan, had entered the war and British troops had not engaged the enemy in the field since the humiliating evacuation of Dunkirk. The tide was however, beginning to turn. In retrospect, perhaps the decisive moments had come in 1941. The early momentum of Operation Barbarossa, launched that year (22 June), gradually dissipated and was finally reversed at Stalingrad, where the frozen and desolate German divisions suffered abject defeat and surrendered on 2 February 1943; it was a triumph of the Russian will. Meanwhile, Hitler had fatefully declared war on the United States within days of the Japanese assault on Pearl Harbour (7 December 1941).

From an allied perspective, 1942 emerged as the year in which the war began to change fundamentally in character, from a 'series of defensive operations'[45] to taking the offensive. Britain gradually moved beyond the counter-measures in response to the U-boat war and stolid aerial resistance of the Battle of Britain to a more aggressive posture; this shift in emphasis was facilitated by a crucial advance in intelligence — the breaking of the German 'ultra' code. In March 1942, bomber command launched the first of its controversial thousand-bomber raids (on Lübeck); the campaign culminated in attacks on Berlin and finally three devastating bombardments on Dresden. Meanwhile on 23 October 1942, British forces registered their first major victory over the Axis army at El Alamein.

Inevitably, these changes transformed Northern Ireland's function within the war effort. The balance of its industrial output gradually shifted from the production of defensive to offensive instruments of war. Its vital strategic role in counteracting a direct German assault diminished. Though an attempt at an Irish invasion was still considered possible, by late 1942 its likelihood had receded almost to vanishing point. However, the region did retain its pivotal position in the Battle of the Atlantic. It also developed as a valuable training ground, collection point and launching pad for allied troops prior to some of the great military offensives in the European and North African theatres. Over 300,000 allied service personnel saw wartime duty in Northern Ireland; north American forces comprised by far the largest non-British component.[46]

The Arrival of American Troops

During early 1941, confidential discussions had begun regarding the possible formation of Vth (US) army corps bases in Northern Ireland and Scotland. The vital initiative came on 23 December (three weeks after Pearl Harbour), when Roosevelt wrote to Churchill agreeing that US units take over Ulster's 'defence, thus freeing British troops for deployment elsewhere',[47] whilst they themselves completed their military training. From late October, the Prime Minister had favoured this course of action, as it would act as a 'powerful additional deterrent' against German invasion of Ireland, especially if the 'actual number' of men involved was magnified.[48] It was not thought that it would 'conflict with [American] preparations for North Africa'[49] and it would release the four UK divisions in the province for service in the Middle and Far East. Moreover, it paralleled an agreement reached (July 1941) whereby the American government had assumed responsibility for the defence of Iceland. On 7 January, John Andrews was summoned unexpectedly to London and two days later attended a meeting of the war cabinet at which details regarding the imminent arrival of large numbers of US troops was disclosed.[50] It was a milestone in the course of the war and in the history of Anglo-American relations.

Already, a nucleus of Vth Army divisions had assembled at Camp Beauregard, Louisiana, and had begun embarkation in New York on 6 January 1942; on the 23rd their first officers arrived in Belfast. At 12.15pm on the 26th a token force of 3,900 men (mainly of the 34th US infantry division) disembarked from the *Chateau Thierry* and *Strathaird* at Dufferin Quay, Belfast. They were welcomed ashore by the strains of the *Star Spangled Banner* (the US national anthem since 1931) played by the band of the Royal Ulster Rifles. The first enlisted man to step ashore officially, and thus the first GI officially to set foot in Europe in World War Two (between 1942-5, three million US forces personnel passed through the United Kingdom) was Private 1st Class, 34th infantryman, Milburn Henke of Hutchinson, Minnesota. He was, ironically, a naturalised German, the youngest soldier of his rank and eventually received 'a fan mail' of 300 letters and cards. The official welcoming ceremony was somewhat upstaged by the fact that another tender had shortly beforehand discharged its contingent of troops at Pollock Dock, and 500 of these were marching past as Henke

A detachment of U.S. troops on Londonderry's west bank, passing one of the city's historic gates
Imperial War Museum; via David Ashe

stepped on to the quayside. The oldest member of the group was Staff Sergeant David Meskimen, a veteran of the Great War who landed with his son, also a sergeant.[51]

The arrival of these units stimulated considerable media attention. One GI, asked by a BBC interviewer if 'this country [was] anything like what you expected?', replied 'Well, we always heard that Ireland was a land of potato famine and that a lot of people left...to come to the States, but ... I'm quite surprised to find....plenty of food and plenty of attractive girls. This is rather important.'[52] Their disembarkation was also given widespread coverage in the American press. The *Daily Oklahoman* (27 January 1942) noted that there was 'no flamboyant welcome. The secret was apparently well kept'. In fact, London had been concerned that 'in spite of the elaborate attempts at secrecy, the common topic of conversation in Eire, as well as in Ulster, was [the troops'] expected arrival.[53] '(The Dublin government had not been officially informed but, from June 1941, garda crime branch operating in the north provided it with very detailed and accurate information on all American and British military movements and preparations until the

February 1942: a contingent of US troops, led by their officers, march into Duke Street having crossed the Craigavon Bridge, Londonderry, following disembarkation at the city's port
Imperial War Museum; via David Ashe

final stages of the war).[54] The local press reported seeing enemy reconnaissance aircraft overhead; German government files indicate that it was in fact the Luftwaffe's last recorded flight over Belfast.The newly arrived American forces initially adopted the roles which had been first assumed by the 53rd (Welsh) division in mid-1940. These were now defined as 'to defend Northern Ireland against the axis powers and to be prepared to move into southern Ireland for the defence thereof'.[55] In early 1942, both the British and the United States government shared residual fears that Germany might still attempt a direct attack on Eire, which Irish sources suggested could not be delayed for more than 48 hours. The American leadership resented southern neutrality: Roosevelt regarded it as 'a serious impediment to the war effort'. When Robert Brennan (Ireland's minister in Washington) informed him of the 'increasing belief on the part of his government and people that these American troops were going to be used to attack Irish forces', Roosevelt's private response was 'that he only wished he could'. Even the pocket guide to Northern Ireland issued to GIs in 1942 stated categorically that de Valera's war policy represented a real danger to the

Disembarkation complete, 26 January 1942, American troops at Belfast docks await transportation to training camps
Belfast Telegraph

allied cause. Plans were quickly devised to neutralise the resulting risk; by mid-April 1942 the presidential envoy, Harry Hopkins, claimed that the GIs 'had it all taped, in the event of an invasion, to occupy Dublin .... in seventy minutes'. The intelligence officer with the proposed strike force expected only 'token resistance' from the Irish army but predicted 'guerrilla' resistance. He advocated that priests should be put under 'immediate surveillance' and there should be 'no fraternisation between the troops and the civil population' because 'under these conditions the Southern Irish are the most treacherous people on earth'.[56]

Primarily, between 1942 and 1944 Northern Ireland served as a crucially important American base for naval and air operations, and also as a holding area and training ground for successive waves of GIs. By late May 1942, troop numbers first peaked at almost 37,000 prior to their participation in 'Operation Torch' against Axis forces in North Africa and Italy. It then subsided until preparations began for the opening up of a second front in western Europe. In June 1944, immediately prior to the Normandy landings it had reached over 120,000 and included units of the XV Corps — 2nd, 5th and 8th infantry and 82nd airborne. This figure represented almost one tenth of the total indigenous population of the six counties from the 1937 census; in Fermanagh where the 8th infantry was deployed it was nearer to one fifth.

American military and civilian personnel relax in a mess hall at Langford Lodge, Co. Antrim
Belfast Telegraph

An impressive infrastructure was rapidly established (by 1943) to accommodate the American presence; it included numerous airfields (18 were in operation at the end of the war), many military camps and barracks and other diverse naval and air facilities. From late June 1941, up to 1,500 US technicians had been based in Northern Ireland to begin preparations. Possibly the most unusual logistical problem which they confronted was the reluctance of some local people to remove 'fairy thorn bushes from the middle of proposed runways in Fermanagh'.[57] All around Newry, trenches were dug and fortifications erected for military training. Almost certainly the most impressive development was the construction of a virtual new town at Langford Lodge, the early nineteenth-century family home of Sir Hercules Pakenham, sited on the shores of Lough Neagh. When completed in 1942, it served as an aircraft repair depot for the Lockheed Overseas Corporation, the American firm nominated by the United States government to operate it; on 15 August it was officially designated as United States Air Force base 597. During construction it had legitimately been described as 'the fastest growing suburb of L.A.';[58] a US press report suggested in January 1944 that 'there [had] never been anything like it since the Pilgrim Fathers went the other way'.[59] At peak, it accommodated 6,000 inhabitants. It employed 2,200 Irish civilian personnel by December 1943 (US employers expected a

Civilian employees alight at Gortnagallon railway station on their way to Langford Lodge
Belfast Telegraph

higher output per worker per hour, than locals were used to providing). Its facilities included a medical unit, fire department, laundry, library, independent telephone system, daily newspaper and cinema. In total, its workforce was responsible for modifying 3,250 and servicing 11,000 aircraft, repairing countless damaged planes and overhauling 450,000 components. British troops were employed to guard the millions of dollars worth of machinery and supplies required; although little sabotage occurred, fears were intense.

Meanwhile, Londonderry's potential as a naval base was more fully exploited; in April 1941, the US Navy had made arrangements with the British government to build four bases, two in the six counties (the second was to be at Lough Erne), and two in Scotland (at Rosneath and Loch Ryan). The first overt sign of an American presence came as early as 30 June 1941, when almost 400 US technical personnel arrived by ship. As the United States was still neutral, they wore civilian clothes; many were so gaudily dressed that onlookers at first assumed there were women in the contingent. Their first impressions tended to centre on the lack of night life and the weather. One of the first to arrive quipped that the city was like a 'cemetery with electric light'.[60] Another, depressed by the constant rain, claimed that its barrage balloon defences were really designed to keep the place from sinking. Whatever local people thought of their humour, they certainly marvelled at their technology and industry. The first US naval servicemen to arrive in the British Isles, after Pearl Harbour, disembarked at Londonderry from the trawler *Albatross* on 18 January 1942. By February 1942, garda crime branch described the city as 'like an American port'.[61] During 1942-3, $75 million was expended, mainly in the vicinity of the port; massive facilities for the repair, maintenance and fuelling of escort vehicles were constructed. United States naval headquarters was established in January 1942 at Talbot House, near Magee College. It contained a heavily fortified bunker which would have become the control centre for North West Approaches Command had the base at Derby House, Liverpool, been bombed. A naval radio station for communication with Atlantic shipping was also established there — the most important US station in the European theatre. Another was established at Clooney Park which continued to operate until 1977, being used in later years to transmit the 'hot line' signal, linking Washington and Moscow, via Whitehall. At peak, in April 1943, a total of 149 ships were based in Londonderry (including 30 destroyers) helping to protect the western approaches and crewed by over 20,000 sailors. Initially most were American; they continued to use the facilities until August 1944, but from late 1943 the naval craft and personnel were predominantly British or Canadian, with the Free French, Free Dutch, Free Norwegian, Polish,

THE AMERICAN PARACHUTE INFANTRY ARE CORDIALLY INVITED TO A . . . . .

DANCE

IN ROYAL NAVAL HALL, 58 ROYAL AVE. ON TUESDAY 29th FEBRUARY. 1944, given by

W. R. N. S.
BELFAST.

Russian and Commonwealth marines well represented. In this period, the combined total of all forces strength in the city probably exceeded 40,000; its population therefore approximately doubled. The overall strategic significance of the north-west was enhanced, not only by Coastal Command's use of neighbouring airports but also by the construction for the American navy from January 1942 of a substantial timber jetty at Lisahally, on the right bank of the Foyle (for unloading and fuelling escort ships).[62]

Relations between US Forces and the People of Northern Ireland

Inevitably, friction did from time to time arise between such large numbers of U.S. forces personnel and the host population. The unenviable distinction of being the first American serviceman to be court-martialled in the United Kingdom during the war fell to a sergeant who was in the scout car escorting an army convoy on the road from Limavady to Londonderry on 17 April 1942. Amongst those in the vehicles following were US army's Chief of

Children chasing after the first contingent of U.S. troops to disembark in Belfast, 26 January 1942
David Ashe, Langford Lodge Wartime Centre

Staff, General C. Marshall, Roosevelt's personal envoy, Harry Hopkins, the roving Lend-Lease 'Ambassador', Averell Harriman, Lieutenant-General Cheney, commanding the US army in the United Kingdom and Major- General Hartle, commanding USA NIF. Near Ballykelly an incident occurred in which a bus driver was shot dead; it was alleged that he had deliberately delayed the motorcade by holding to the middle of the road. Sergeant W.V. Clipsham forced his way past and fired three shots into the cab when level. The bus careered into a bridge; death was instantaneous. Clipsham was tried for manslaughter but in effect exonerated by an exclusively American inquiry on the basis of technical evidence. Almost certainly he had thought that he was being deliberately cut off from the convoy in order to set up an IRA attack. The incident caused widespread ill feeling in the area especially amongst the local protestant population; garda crime branch described the victim as having been 'a very bigoted Orangeman'.[63] Subsequently Londonderry was declared out of bounds to all US troops.

More generally, there were some American behavioural characteristics which did cause comment and on occasion friction in Ulster. The GIs were better educated and more sophisticated than the native population and on occasions could give the impression of 'knowing it all', so infuriating the local people. As Tom Harrisson noted, however, this 'attitude' contrasted with the fact that the Irish found them 'easy people to fleece'. A further potential source of conflict was the high pay and overall affluence of the GIs which, though they were generous, caused local resentment and bitterness and even some 'natural grumbling on the part of British troops'.[64] On 8 August 1942 they were instructed 'to refrain from encouraging begging'[65] in Belfast. Predictably, much of their income was spent on alcohol; by June 1942 a 'leading' Belfast consultant reported '3 cases of Americans dead as a result of drink'. Alternative forms of entertainment for them were frequently lacking - hotels crowded, newspapers and radio programmes incomprehensible, films dated and sports facilities unsuitable or non-existent. Their consumption of liquor might well leave supplies for neighbouring civilians short, cause aggressive or insensitive behaviour and lead to arguments over local girls. Harrisson noted: 'Most of the women liked Americans, and this in itself coupled with the amount of money they had to spend...is bound to upset some of the native men'.[66]

The 'Protestant Sunday' enforced throughout Ulster was especially resented by the US troops; it was 'a place of the dead on [their]...traditional day of fun'; some 'escaped' by crossing the border to Donegal or even travelling to Dublin. On weekdays, Belfast 'compared favourably' with most places from the seamen's viewpoint, but in Londonderry recreational

American Ways

facilities were poor and inadequate. In June 1942, Harrisson wrote: 'This little country town has suddenly become a humming centre of shipping and seamen of all sorts. The limited existing entertainment facilities are overloaded... The main novelty is a number of pinball arcades... places of the poorest type, dirty, with blaring music through gramophone and loud speakers, gambling slot machines, competition shooting galleries and an open form of roulette ... [in] flagrant violation of the gaming laws... . Very large sums are taken in this game every evening when the arcades are packed. The most popular is directly in front of the police station'. Drinking was the other main occupation ('pubs and pick-ups'), with Londonderry the focus of illicit whiskey smuggling, and much poteen being brought across the border.[67] There are other examples of entrepreneurial enterprise; in 1943 local newspapers recorded the conviction of three of the city's citizens for operating 'disorderly houses'.[68]

A further cause of friction was the fact that a small proportion of the US soldiers was black and some local evidence suggests that for a time 'racial violence replaced sectarian violence'.[69] In Northern Ireland on occasion the issue assumed a sectarian tinge. A Unionist MP complained (in Co. Londonderry) that the girls going out with black GIs were 'mostly of the lowest type and belong to our minority'.[70] An anonymous, undated letter written by a black GI to the members of the Northern Ireland government gives a stark impression of the level of racial prejudice he experienced in the province. The anti-black feeling which he experienced was shown not only by some local people but was also visible in the behaviour of British soldiers and sailors and, above all, of white members of United States forces. He wrote:

Dear Sirs,

I am an American, coloured, soldier. My group of fellows have been stationed here in Antrim for 9 months. We are trying to do our part in the fight for freedom, but since we have been here we have met so much sergregation [sic], prejudice and strife. Some time we doubt the allied cause.

We are stationed near Antrim, located in the town, at the establishments of Hall's and Murphy's. They are hotel owners. In visiting these establishments, we have been sergregated. To describe one incident, a friend and I visited Hall's, they refused to serve us because we are coloured. Dear Sir, you and I both know that regardless of colour, we are all human. We come to Ireland not because we wanted to, but we came to do our part in this war. Since being here we have gained the respect of the people of Ireland.

One town in particular is Carrickfergus. We were there for five weeks and I can assure you that we were perfect gentlemen. When we left the people cried; they want us to stay there. The people of that town is giving us a party on the 23rd of this month. Sir, for the people like us then we must be gentlemen. The wee kids here they cried for us to return to them. We visit them at every opportunity. The people are always glad to see us. If we treat the people nice, then they should treat us the same. I believe that you are a man of justice and I think that you believe is right.

Regardless to where a man is born or regardless to his colour, every man has his right to enjoy life here on this earth. Just because I am a dark man doesn't mean that I am not intelligent. The anatomy of the white man is the same as the dark man. God created all men as brother, and my belief is that since we are all here in Ireland we should live as brothers and sisters and not as enemies. We hate to walk the streets of Belfast merely because we are insulted. They use the words 'nigger' and 'darky'. Those are two words that we hate. Those words were brought here by the American whites. The American whites taught the people those words in order to start strife and envy among the people and us. The Americans are the lowest breed of the human race. They fear us because of our ability to advance in knowledge. We want to be friends of the Irish, not enemies. We want the people to like us not hate us. If your people visit Africa, or some dark continent, they would be treated as human.

The first black American troops to arrive in Northern Ireland line up in formation at the docks in Belfast, before going to camp, 14 July 1942
David Ashe, Langford Lodge Wartime Centre

Sir, will you try your influence on the people? To show our love for the Irish children, our battalion raised a fund to support an Irish orphan for five years. We love the children and they love us. As I walked through the streets of Ireland, accepting insults, I sometime wonder if the people are ignorant to the fact that they are insulting us. Please try your influence to correct the people on these errors. Print it in the paper that we are coloured Americans not niggers or darkies. Lately we have had fights with British sailors and soldiers. They call us Black Bastards, son-of-bitches. We take these to a certain degree. Carrickfergus is the only town in Northern Ireland that we like because when we visited there we are treated like human. I believe all Irish are kind. I would reveal my name but if I did the American Authorities would Court Martial me. They don't like the truth.

I close in the name of the God of all men

A coloured soldier[71]

As the letter suggests much of prejudice and tension which did arise locally was between members of the US forces themselves. At the time, another black soldier wondered whether he had been sent overseas 'to fight our white soldiers or against the Nazis'.[72] A white lieutenant had felt it 'necessary [in his own words] to lay down the law to the Irish and the coons',[73] while a corporal bleakly claimed that 'civil war' had started among the American troops in Ireland. A white quartermaster shed some further light on the cause of the ill-feeling, commenting, 'It seems that several outfits of coloured troops preceded us over here and have succeeded pretty well in salting away the local feminine pulchritude... The girls really go for them in preference to the white boys, a fact that irks the boys no end'.[74] On 30 September 1942,

USAAF Army and Navy personnel outside theAmerican Red Cross Club, (formerly the Plaza Ballroom) opened on 6 June 1942
David Ashe, Langford Lodge Wartime Centre

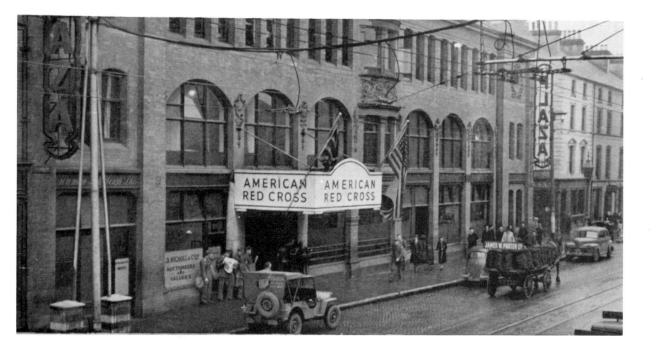

black and white troops had clashed in Antrim, leaving one black GI dead and a white colleague wounded; possibly it was this incident which prompted the author to write his anonymous letter. Earlier, in September, Brooke recorded travelling to London for discussions with British officials on the 'coloured question'.[75] One solution adopted by US officers themselves in the province was to encourage covert racial segregation. In August 1943, 'Rules of Good Conduct' were drawn up on General Hartle's initiative, as GOC. These advocated total segregation where possible - separate accommodation and separate dances and private parties. It included the admonition 'Neither race must interfere with or cut in on soldiers of the other race in company with girls'.[76]

In general, however, Harrisson was struck by the 'noteworthy lack of friction from the outset' (June 1942) between the American troops and the civilian population in Northern Ireland; he thought it 'much less than might have been anticipated'. He concluded that overall the US forces' morale was 'high' and in many respects 'higher' than that of English troops in Ulster. He described attending a typical Saturday evening dance at the Guildhall in Londonderry; he considered that the behaviour of the American soldiers and sailors was 'excellent...unimpeachable' and that 'relations between them, the British troops, the few Irish men and numerous Irish women present [an estimated 50% from Eire] was normal and agreeable'.[77] Essentially, the US troops were difficult to dislike: they were characteristically cheerful, lively, amiable, casually clothed with an easy manner, an appealing informality of discipline and a lack of obvious distinction between officers and men. Elements of their behaviour proved contagious - notably, the playing of poker and dice, chewing gum, jitterbugging; in Fermanagh 'local men got used to smoking Camel and Lucky Strike'.[78] Generally the management of local dancehalls, cinemas and hotels throughout the north competed eagerly for their custom; in Belfast horse-drawn carriages were improvised as taxis by local entrepreneurs to meet their demand in the context of strict petrol rationing. Considerable efforts were made to counteract any feelings of cultural isolation or impoverishment. There were visits not only by generals, including Eisenhower (July 1942) and Patton (March 1944), but also leading entertainers. Al Jolson and Glenn Miller played at Langford Lodge in 1942 and 1944 respectively; others included Bob Hope, Irving Berlin and the boxer, Joe Louis.

The large number of inter-allied marriages suggests a high level of social integration. The GIs were advised, before leaving the States, that army regulations were being relaxed to permit them to marry without obtaining permission from their commanding officer. The first wedding took place on 13 April 1942, in College Square Presbyterian church, between Private H.W.

Cooke of Cleveland, Ohio, and Miss Thelma Smith from Belfast. As many as 1,800 more followed, though soldiers were offered no special privileges and the authorities made it clear that wives would not automatically receive American citizenship and that their voyage to the USA would not be at the US government's expense. This last condition threatened hardship unless the local families concerned had sufficient private means. After the war the *Belfast Telegraph* backed the 'forgotten GI wives campaign' which claimed that Northern Ireland girls were bring treated with less consideration than their English counterparts in being re-united with their husbands in the United States. Eventually in 1946, the US government relented and sent the 12,000 ton coverted troop ship *Henry Gibbons* to Belfast for the first consignment of 445 brides; several weeks later a further 219 crossed over on the *James Park*. John Cole, then in his first year of reporting for the *Belfast Telegraph* covered the story under the headline *Sighs, Smiles, Tears as Bride Ship Sails*.[79]

Arnie and Caroline Yates: an American Officer with his Ulster bride, outside Eglinton Presbyterian Church, Carr's Glen, Belfast
Belfast Telegraph

On the whole, Harrisson's favourable impression of local GI morale in 1942 seems to have been sustained throughout the war; 'where sectarianism could be negotiated' they appear to have been 'most at home' in Ulster. This was the conclusion reached by Iphigene Bettman, a US official who toured around the US bases throughout the United Kingdom, during 1943-4. Many of the troops told her that 'hospitality in Ulster was second to none, even in America'. The official system of hospitality, organised from the outset with great enthusiasm by Sir Basil Brooke, was more smoothly coordinated and higher powered than in Britain; Brooke's committee arranged fishing and factory visits, with regular dances and home hospitality most popular. Bettman's report concluded: 'the strain is obviously here in England, where reserve, formality and trace of 'superior race' feeling makes the difference of our custom a greater cause of friction'.[80] Another US survey concluded that the American soldier lacked 'the desired respect for the British'. On a visit to Belfast after the war, Eisenhower echoed some of these sentiments; he stated 'I have received honours in a number of cities but never have been more impressed with the sincerity and friendliness exhibited towards me than in Belfast'. He also paid warm tribute to the province's wartime role, observing that: 'without Northern Ireland, I do not see how the American forces could have been concentrated to begin the invasion of Europe'.[81]

General Eisenhower inspecting troops in front of the City Hall, Belfast, 24 August 1945. He received the Freedom of the City
Public Record Office of Northern Ireland

6
WIDER STILL AND WIDER
NORTHERN IRELAND, BRITAIN AND EIRE
1939-1945

Relations between Westminister and Stormont

The first priority of Brooke's government after taking office had been to improve the relationship between Britain and Northern Ireland and so strengthen the union. With the end of the war in sight, Sir Basil expressed the 'hope that you [Britain] now realize that we are necessary to you'.[1] His wish was fully realized. Northern Ireland's wartime role did win the gratitude of British ministers (and possibly voters), transformed their assessment of its strategic significance to Britain and measurably influenced their policies towards the region both during and after the war. An early and important indication of this was the presence of and the speech delivered by George VI when he addressed both houses of parliament at Stormont on 18 July 1945; it was an occasion from which Brooke derived immense pride and satisfaction. In his comments the King acknowledged that the friendship shown to the United States troops based in the province had done 'much to strengthen' Anglo-American relations. He spoke of their shared experience of the recent conflict, noting, 'Your homes have not escaped the ravages of war. ... your shipyards, your fields, your factories have been of splendid service to the common cause'. He expressed his gratitude for having the 'opportunity of personally thanking the people of Northern Ireland'.[2] Twenty-four years earlier when his father, George V, had opened this same parliament (in Belfast's City Hall) he had referred in measured terms throughout to the 'six counties' — not to 'Northern Ireland'.[3] Now in 1945, in the aftermath of war, this calculated ambiguity and implicit lack of commitment to partition had vanished.

Some leading politicians in Britain reiterated King George VI's views, and drew lessons for future policy from the recent past. In September 1945, Lord Jowitt (wartime Minister of National Insurance) declared 'Britain has gone through six perilous years of war with Ulster at her side, and I do not want to visualize any future unless Ulster is still at her side'.[4] Churchill spoke in similar vein. In 1943, he had written: 'But for the loyalty of Northern

Ireland and its devotion to what has now become the cause of thirty governments or nations, we should have been confronted with slavery and death and the light which now shines so brightly throughout the world would have been quenched'.[5] Looking to the future, in 1945, he stated: 'a strong, loyal Ulster will always be vital to the security and well-being of our whole empire'.[6] At the time, it was not clear how or whether such sentiments would in practice influence future policy at Westminster, particularly if the wartime 'swing to the left' resulted in a post-war majority Labour government.

Westminster's appreciation of Northern Ireland's wartime role was related closely to and vastly inflated by its parallel sense of irritation with the policies adopted by the Dublin government throughout the conflict. In fact, Eire's position had been one of benevolent anti-German neutrality. After their discussions in 1940, Malcolm MacDonald wrote that de Valera 'could scarcely have provided more benevolent cooperation short of declaring war against the enemy'.[7] Eduard Hempel even complained of the anti-German bias of Irish newspapers — especially the *Irish Press*, which was closest to the government (he was quite satisfied with the content and tone of the *Irish Independent*).[8] Within Ireland, this characteristic was demonstrated most dramatically by the assistance provided by southern firemen after the Belfast blitz. More generally, it was illustrated by, for example, the liaison between allied and Irish military authorities on plans for Ireland's defence (the precise extent is disputed), cooperation between G2 (southern intelligence) and allied intelligence services (on IRA activity, etc), the exchange of meteorological reports, the forwarding to Britain on request of information (on an almost daily basis) about the movement of Axis planes, ships and submarines in the Irish Sea and permission (from January 1941) for allied aircraft to overfly a corridor over Co. Donegal, west of Lough Erne. In addition, German servicemen who made forced landings or crashed inside Irish territorial waters or territory were generally interned, while allied personnel were repatriated. The British legation in Dublin had two wireless transmitters and a private telephone line to both London and Belfast, while Hempel was forced to hand over his one transmitter to the Irish authorities. At the time, December 1943, he protested to Dublin ministers that, despite their professed neutrality, they were treating Britain more leniently than Germany. Moreover, more than 100,000 Irish men and women worked without restriction in British munitions factories in wartime, and upwards of 60,000 enlisted in crown forces, either across the border or in England. In Belfast, for instance, 28,654 Eire citizens joined the army, 9,426 the RAF and 4,893 the Royal Navy. Approximately 5,000 non-commissioned officers and other ranks from the Irish army broke the terms of their commissions to join British forces or to take up civilian employment in the United Kingdom by June 1945. The southerners who entered military service in wartime won, in total, 780 decorations, including 8 Victoria Crosses — Canada, with three times the population of the 26 counties, won 10. In addition, the two governments cooperated in, for instance, making combined purchases of wheat, maize, sugar and livestock fodder and in the importation and allocation of petrol. Moreover the south provided Britain with its entire food surplus. Arguably, at no time since 1922 had the London and Dublin administrations cooperated together so closely.[9]

At the same time, however, in spite of acute allied pressure, powerful inducements — including the offer of Irish unity — and for a time the imminent prospect of fascist victory, de Valera pursued a policy of strict neutrality over a succession of vital issues. As a result, he exasperated both the United Kingdom and American governments. Thus, both John Maffey and David Gray, representatives in Dublin of the respective administrations, claimed from time to time that his neutrality policy was working to Germany's advantage.

For instance, de Valera denied the allies use of Irish ports and airfields from the outset of war. He refused entry to British troops, in May 1940, in advance of German invasion, and rejected the bait of Irish unity. He protested that the arrival of US troops in the north (January 1942) was an 'unwarranted interference' in his nation's affairs, a violation of its sovereignty and represented an implicit sanctioning of partition;[10] he also complained that he had not been consulted by either Britain or the United States (the IRA similarly described it as an 'unjustifiable occupation').[11] David Gray asked why 'he [the Taoiseach] protested American troops coming as friends for the protection of Ireland and did not protest German bombers coming to bomb Belfast and kill Irish nationals'.[12] In February 1944, he rejected forceful American requests that the Axis representative in Ireland be expelled as 'constituting a danger to the lives of [our] soldiers' and allied operations (D Day was approaching).[13] Instead, he placed the Irish army on alert, warned the public that 'war may come upon us'[14] and called an election, so exploiting the boost to his popularity. Later that year, in September, he was unwilling to give American officials assurances that asylum would not be granted to Axis war criminals.

Before hostilities had ceased, Anglo-Irish relations suffered a further major reversal when, on 2 May 1945, de Valera chose to visit the German minister in Dublin, Eduard Hempel, at the legation in 53 Northumberland Road to offer his condolences on the death of Hitler. Hempel's response is not clear; certainly at Iveagh House (the Irish foreign ministry) he was not considered to be a Nazi but rather a professional career diplomat. At the time, newspapers were full of revelations about Belsen and Buchenwald. The

Irish government defended the action as being no more than the 'diplomatic minimum'[15] and urged that it had marked Roosevelt's death (15 April 1945) much more effusively. In the United States, the Taoiseach's action made front page news; the *New York Herald Tribune*'s headline was *Neutrality Gone Mad*.[16] Both in Washington and London consideration was given to withdrawing their respective ambassadors in protest, but instead both chose to deliver a severe reprimand.

Overall, as one Westminster official observed, had Britain lost the war its relationship with Ireland would probably have been irretrievably damaged. Occasionally throughout the war, Churchill had expressed his exasperation with Eire's policy. During the conscription discussions, in May 1941, he had told the Irish High Commissioner in London, J. W. Dulanty, that his 'blood boiled at the attitude of Ireland today'; she was keeping out of the war 'for the most ignoble of reasons of not being bombed',[17] in what was in essence a conflict between good and evil. One week after VE Day (on 13 May), he gave full vent to his government's accumulated sense of grievance; Ulster was the clear beneficiary of his frustration and anger. He stated: 'This was indeed a deadly moment in our lives and if it had not been for the loyalty and friendship of Northern Ireland, we should have been forced to come to close quarters with Mr de Valera or perish forever from the earth'.[18] After due consideration, on 16 May, the Taoiseach replied; he observed that Churchill's views, 'if accepted, would mean that Britain's necessity would become a moral code,' in which 'other people's rights did not count.'[19] While this may be dismissed as a naive view, given the context of total war, at the time Maffey considered that he had 'found the authentic anti-British note' and 'did not put a foot wrong.'[20]

Even before the war was over, Stormont ministers had already reaped one reward for their supportive wartime role, and it was of the utmost future significance. Partly in response to electoral pressure, they had become acutely anxious to maintain parity of social services with Britain in peacetime, to implement fully the terms of the Beveridge report and to begin the process of catching up with provision elsewhere in the United Kingdom in such vital areas of social welfare as education and housing. However, such a programme would require a substantial increase in public spending and this implied a fundamental re-examination of the hitherto unsatisfactory financial relationship between Stormont and Westminster. Local officials regarded the winter of 1943 as an opportune moment to initiate preliminary negotiations, aimed at ensuring that their departments had sufficient funds. Spender observed that there had been a general loosening in the recent budgetary policy of the imperial government. Also he noted that relations with Treasury officials were friendly, that the Chancellor was sympathetic and that even socialist members of the war cabinet were by then appreciative of Ulster's wartime efforts. By early 1944, the basis of a future agreement had been laid which guaranteed Northern Ireland ministers adequate financial support from the Exchequer to meet all Ulster's reasonable expenditure. Already, in November 1943, Maynard Sinclair, Minister of Finance, advised the Commons that: 'the imperial authorities [would] give sympathetic consideration to the case for special measures, as regards any service in which Northern Ireland has leeway to make up in order to obtain equality of standard with the United Kingdom'.[21] The Treasury's willingness to raise its level of financial support, after its relative niggardliness during the inter-war years, owed much to the sympathy generated by the shared experience of war. The successful outcome of the negotiations was a defining moment in the history of the province. It formed the basis for the region's transformation after 1945, and was the foundation stone for its best years — the 1950s and early 1960s.

Inter-Government Relations in Ireland

Meanwhile, relations between the governments and peoples within Ireland itself showed no comparable improvement. A 'cold war' had existed between Belfast and Dublin from the early 1920s, and subsequently the political, economic and cultural gap had widened, especially after de Valera became Taoiseach in 1932. Southern neutrality did much to reinforce partition — it contributed significantly to the British government's new-found commitment to Northern Ireland. It was both symptom and cause of the breach opening up between London and Dublin. This was further evidenced by de Valera's comment in November 1945. 'Eire is a Republic, an independent sovereign republic... King George is not our King'.[22] He did not, however, sever Ireland completely from the Commonwealth. Neutrality also deepened the chasm in experience and identity between north and south. Brooke regarded it with contempt and disdain; it seemed proof of his frequent claim that though 'the border was a border of stones and ditches . . . it merely represented a division of thought and hearts and heads'.[23] The growing wartime contrast in conditions north and south stimulated not just the smuggling of goods, but also an increased flow of people. Thousands of southerners migrated north to seek work. The south became a favourite wartime retreat for thousands of northerners. In 1941, they crossed the border fleeing from the terror of the blitz; but this apart they came mainly to escape the privations and restrictions of the war. For Unionists, the experience was perhaps less likely to undermine their political faith than heighten their awareness of the differences between the two parts of the island.

The sterile cold war relationship between north and south received one substantial jolt in the course of the conflict. In 1941, de Valera proved willing on two occasions to dispatch southern firemen to Belfast in response to requests for help from the Northern government, after successive German air-raids. There had always been discreet inter-governmental cooperation, usually conducted through officials over a wide range of rather mundane issues, including fisheries, transport, labour recruitment, agriculture and land drainage. But the assistance provided during the blitz (along with obviously genuine expressions of sympathy by southern leaders and the hospitality shown to northern evacuees) made a deeply favourable impression on both northern officials and people; the *Irish Times* claimed that the 'working class districts' were especially appreciative. [24] It was a spontaneous open, dramatic and generous gesture. It briefly raised the prospect, amongst some of the public at least, of a new era in cross-border cooperation and friendship. John Maffey advised the Dublin leadership that the Stormont government was 'extremely appreciative' of southern assistance and added that 'an extraordinary amount of good...was bound to come from this gesture'.[25]

The decision to send assistance north was de Valera's, possibly after discussion with J. P. Walshe, his foreign affairs minister. On the first occasion, the Taoiseach recalled receiving the request for help at about 1:50 am on 16 April and that he 'spent a few minutes considering'[26] it, before giving his consent. Major Comerford, chief superintendent of Dublin Fire Brigade, was instructed to dispatch aid to the north within 20 minutes of the original telephone call from Belfast. By the time a conference of ministers had assembled in the early hours of the morning to discuss the matter, the 'all clear' had already been given to the fire brigade. It caused some controversy in the south. Professor T.D. Rudmose Brown, Trinity College, Dublin wrote to de Valera, saying that it was 'insane to irritate the Germans' as he had done, that assisting the north was 'endangering our neutrality' and that this policy should be persisted with 'even at the risk of starvation'.[27] And indeed Lord Haw-Haw did make some ominous references to it on the wireless; there had been occasional veiled threats to Eire on German radio since 1939, warning, for example, that she 'had better come out from Mr Chamberlain's umbrella'.[28] Eduard Hempel, however, was reassuring; the minutes of the southern Ministry of External Affairs stated: 'the reports in the English papers that the German Minister protested strongly against our action as a breach of neutrality were completely false. In fact, [he] regarded it as only natural that we should send help to our own people.'[29]

But even southern aid during the blitz generated controversy and bitterness. Opposition MPs at Stormont alleged that the government failed adequately to acknowledge its debt or express publicly its gratitude for the help received. This criticism was without substance. Nonetheless, such open collaboration with the Dublin leadership had certainly been forced upon northern ministers by the tragic and extreme circumstances of the blitz: they regarded the request for aid from de Valera as the 'only course available.'[30] Also, their sentiments of gratitude were undoubtedly diluted by a strong suspicion that the Eire government was, in Spender's phrase, 'utilizing the occasion to indulge in further propaganda for a united Ireland'.[31] Irritation was caused by statements such as de Valera's (on 21 April) that 'they are all our people — we are one and the same people';[32] it was his first public comment about the blitz. This viewpoint also found expression in the southern media; the *Irish Times* commented: 'when all is said and done the people of the six counties are our own folk and blood is stronger than the highest explosives'.[33]

Moreover, northern ministers contended that the un-blacked-out lights of southern cities and towns were consistently used by the Luftwaffe to help identify targets in the six counties. This presumption had undoubted validity. On 29 March 1941, John Maffey informed the Irish government that ...'the latest British air operational developments had made it clear that the lighting of...main towns [in Eire] in the vicinity of the coast were a navigational help to the Germans'.[34] The Dublin government did agree to impose a limited blackout order on 8 April 1941, the day following Belfast's first raid; it applied only to neon street adverts, shop window lighting and cinema exteriors and came into effect on the evening of 15 April — hours before the catastrophic Easter Tuesday attack. A report, produced by Eire's Ministry of Defence (dated 16 July 1941), analysed the effect of 'the lighting in Dublin city and border areas' on the recent blitz in the six counties. It confirmed that Stormont's assertions were not just paranoia. It concluded:

> 'It must be assumed that the lighting in general and that of Dublin city in particular has been used consistently by aircraft for navigational purposes . . . [The Luftwaffe] were apparently using the lights along the coast as an aid to navigation. The consistency with which they approached and touched at certain points made this obvious..... The lights on the south coast and of Dublin were used as points of arrival and departure in synchronized timing.'[35]

These findings confirmed the views of W.P. Delamere, the Chief Officer in Eire's Air Defence Command. On 6 October 1940, he had written a memorandum which concluded... 'I am satisfied that unknown aircraft are making use of the lights of Dublin and other towns at night for navigational purposes'.[36] It was not, however, in the south's security interests to dim them. In November 1941, Joseph Walshe stressed to Eduard Hempel that 'the present lighting of Dublin was a sufficient indication of identity'[37] to the Luftwaffe, as also were the south's shipping lights, and that by implication, therefore, no air raids on southern territory or property could be justified.

Overall, unionist leaders considered that they had every reason to treat the south with extreme caution and wariness. In a number of ways it seemed to represent a direct threat to Northern Ireland's survival; the pressure on Craig to enter into constitutional dialogue with de Valera in 1940 being merely the most overt instance. In May 1940, Brooke warned Craig of the real danger that Germany might invade the south and so threaten Ulster. He advised him to 'watch this possibility', as it would 'enable Hitler to threaten the western approaches to Britain, and was the 'easiest place, in view of IRA activity';[38] also an invading force could exploit anti-English sentiment in Eire. Moreover Andrews was also convinced that, out of deference to southern sensibilities, Westminister provided the province with insufficient protection. The build-up of British troops in the six counties during 1940-41, however, and even of American forces in 1942, would suggest that the opposite was in fact the case.

Ministers and officials at Stormont also regarded the south as a major security risk both to Northern Ireland and to the allied war effort. Spender, for example, assumed that the Dublin government had 'definitely pro-Nazi' sympathies and policies. In May 1941, he recorded in his private diary that this had been illustrated by recent Dail debates; these he alleged, proved that the southern leaders 'had prevented their people from hearing the Vatican's pronouncements against the Nazis. I am afraid,' he added, 'that certain members of the Eire government who have lately received great accessions in their personal wealth must be obtaining it from hostile sources'.[39] Such dark suspicions made any suggestion of Irish unity unthinkable. In 1940, Maffey suggested to Spender that 'If the British Empire were defeated in this war...it would be very greatly to the advantage of Northern Ireland to join up with Eire and that the British government would advise Ulster to do so'. Spender was horrified, replying that 'this was a contingency which I refused to visualize and that I did not think it merited any thought or further discussion'.[40]

Moreover, in common with the British and American governments, the unionist leadership regarded the existence of the Axis legations in Dublin and the constant flow of traffic to and fro across the border as a major security risk, and a significant source of leaked information to the enemy. This was also alleged by the US government in February 1944, when demanding the legation's closure. It claimed that the espionage was 'highly organized' by enemy agents, who had an 'unrestricted opportunity' to collect and collate military information. It concluded that 'neutrality therefore continues to operate in favour of the Axis powers'.[41] In 1942, GIs were advised in their briefing manual, 'spies sift back and forth across the border constantly'.[42] Stormont Home Affairs minister, J. E. Warnock, estimated in November 1944 that 'over 30,000 Eire citizens have applied to come and reside in our midst'[43] since 1940. The northern Ministry of Labour was actively involved in cross-border recruitment, especially to fill vacancies in heavy industry, where local labour supplies were inadequate. Brooke considered that 'It is of course a danger but . . . the war effort is essential and if we are short of men we must get them up.'[44] Andrews, however, was throughout extremely wary of their importation, and it did undoubtedly raise major political and security difficulties. It caused resentment in the north due to the persistence of relatively high levels of unemployment until 1942, and the fact that considerable numbers of Ulster workers had been obliged to transfer to Britain to find work. Also a significant proportion of migrant labour was employed on highly sensitive construction sites and at quarries where explosives were available. In towns such as Newry, local people were convinced that Axis agents were active nearby. One inhabitant recalled that 'Across the border, it was common to meet a chap with a foreign accent and a very close haircut, whom we soon learned [was] German...The German Embassy staff spent a lot of time around Dundalk for very obvious reasons'.[45]

Tom Harrisson considered that cross-border migration did constitute a significant security risk. He observed: 'enemy agents would hardly have to rely on overheard talk in Belfast as there is a large nationalist element working inside the docks . . . and many men from Eire now work in the area, especially at Harland & Wolff and Short & Harland. Many of these men go regularly to and fro across the border.. . . Tongues almost automatically loosen in the neutral atmosphere of Eire'. His enquiries had also convinced him that both groups of workers were to some extent involved in subversive activity and in fomenting labour unrest in Northern industry. He claimed that there was 'undoubtedly a considerable area of fostered dissatisfaction', notably at Short & Harland. Nonetheless, he attributed the 'very unsatisfactory labour relations' there mainly to 'poor management'.[46] Ironically, the Dublin government was also uneasy about the flow of workers to the north-east. It feared, in particular, the economic and political consequences of the simultaneous expulsion of thousands of southern-born workers when the war ended, and more generally that they might have come into contact with and absorbed socialist ideas, whilst away from home.[47]

There is little to suggest that Germany did glean much information through spies or agents operating in Northern Ireland and who were based in the south. The lightly-staffed legations there hardly constituted a formidable phalanx, capable of infiltrating and subverting Irish political life, or of orchestrating migrant labour into an effective intelligence-gathering network.

In February 1944, the US could produce little evidence of espionage. It stated that two German parachutists had been dropped into Eire in 1943 (both had been quickly arrested) and that Hempel was in possession of a wireless transmitter (which the authorities likewise had seized; the German minister was informed by Walshe on 15 December 1943 that it was not acceptable that he should be in possession of such equipment at a time when 'the whole world is talking about a second front').[48] There were also rumours in Washington that the German legation had sent Berlin a detailed report on American military movements in Ulster. Yet despite their existence, Germany received no advance warning of either the North Africa expedition in 1942 or, more crucially, the D Day landings in 1944. Nonetheless, enemy reconnaissance aircraft were there to witness and record the first GIs step ashore in western Europe at Dufferin Quay, in January 1942.

More generally it is almost certain that there was an unquantifiable Irish dimension to other security leaks — most notably those relating to the Dieppe raid, 19 August 1942, and the Arnhem parachute drop of 17 September 1944.[49] In August 1942, Hempel had reported to Berlin that 'retired seamen with a knowledge of the French coast were being called up in England' and that 'Canadians were massed on the south coast of England for a probable invasion of France'. When the 5,000 troops disembarked at Dieppe, the Germans were 'waiting for them'; their casualties aggregated to 3,369. Hempel had gathered his information from various sources, including mainland Britain and it was an 'important element in the allied failure'. There is also evidence that in mid-1944 he learnt of preparations in England for an airborne landing in Holland from a cousin of his friend, Dr Gogan. The absence of a transmitter did not, it seems, prevent the message getting out. This intelligence may account for German success in repulsing the parachute drop at Arnhem. In T. P. Duggan's view, the episode 'gave some substance to Gray's [US minister to Ireland, 1940-1947] arraignments and to Churchill's fears that the security of the Normandy landings could have been imperilled by a last minute leak from Dublin. Messages could get through'. He adds that had Gray, who was extremely critical of Irish neutrality, 'come to know of these messages there would have been no holding him'.[50]

A further case of friction between the two Irish states was Eire's continuing intervention in what Stormont ministers regarded as the north's internal affairs. In the past, this had often been in relation to security issues; however, in wartime, the southern government was taking measures which were at least as firm as those being taken by Stormont, to deal with any possible IRA threat. Nonetheless, de Valera did unsuccessfully plead for clemency in the case of Tom Williams (sentenced to death for his part in a gun battle with police in west Belfast). David Gray complained of the 'glorification' of the convicted man in the south. He noted that 'all over Eire, shops were forcibly closed during the hour of execution by IRA groups or their sympathisers and thousands of people prayed in the streets. He was invested with something of the sanctity of martyrdom'.[51] He compared this response to the apparent indifference displayed by the public in Eire, when republicans were executed there. Dr Herman Goertz, who worked for German intelligence and was parachuted into Ireland in May 1940, also observed that when a Republican was executed in the south 'the population is silent' whereas, when it occurred once in Belfast, 'the shops are shut'.[52] In addition, de Valera had earlier caused much unionist resentment in opposing the introduction of conscription into the six counties and in raising the issue with Westminster, he had reaffirmed: 'their people [ie in Northern Ireland], Catholic and Protestant, are our people'[53] (Ernest Bevin's reply was that the south had signed the treaty and thus accepted partition). When US troops arrived in Northern Ireland, he not only protested at their use of Irish territory (it was, after all, a technical breach of Irish neutrality under articles 2 and 3 of his 1937 constitution), he again asserted Eire's claim to jurisdiction over the whole island, 'no matter what troops occupy the six counties'.[54] A garda crime branch report states that, as a result, GIs were instructed not to go south at any time or under any circumstances so as not to infringe Irish neutrality or sovereignty (the evidence suggests that this injunction was honoured more in the breach than in the observation). Speaking at Stormont, Andrews indignantly repudiated the Taoiseach's right 'to speak in the name of the people of Ireland'.[55]

After the war, the speeches made by Stormont ministers became noticeably more confident and aggressive in tone. Many sought to exploit the south's alleged treachery and perfidy during the conflict and to contrast this with the north's own record; this was projected as one of self-sacrificing devotion and undeviating loyalty to Britain and to the allied cause. Brooke stated in July 1945 that 'if Eire thought that Great Britain was doomed in 1940 and, in consequence, would rather remain neutral, we, on our part, would rather go down with Great Britain than live under any other constitution'.[56] A characteristic post-war unionist publication was entitled: *Eire and the war; de Valera's anti-British Record*. It sought to prove the Taoiseach's consistent bad faith towards the United Kingdom by reference to his uncompromising stance on allied use of the Irish ports, his hostility to US troops coming to the north, his unwillingness to close down the Axis legations or give a commitment that his government would not give asylum to fascist war criminals.[57]

At times it almost seemed to leading Unionists that de Valera played into their hands; the Stormont cabinet found it impossible to predict or even comprehend his decisions. In 1940, for example, Brooke was as surprised as he was relieved that de Valera maintained his strict neutrality policy rather than trade it for unity. He noted in his diary: 'de Valera wants unity with neutrality, an impossible wish. I think this finally cooks his dish'. When he heard of the Taoiseach's response to Hitler's death, he recorded his private thoughts: 'From our point of view his condolences will be most helpful and will strengthen our position enormously. My attitude was — to put it shortly — thank God the man is dead'. He continued: 'I cannot make out de Valera's curious mind. One would have thought he would have tried to come in on the band wagon'.[58] Bewildered or otherwise, Brooke and his party sought to exploit the south's international marginalization. This was preserved post-war by Dublin's perserverance with high tariffs and by its policy of non-alignment towards Europe.

Inter-communal Relations in Northern Ireland

Growing north-south polarization in wartime was paralleled within Northern Ireland by the persistence of deep internal sectarian tensions. The 53rd division found 'many areas . . . very sharply divided politically and on matters of religion. In a few places there existed a degree of hostility between the two rival factions which is unknown in any other parts of the United Kingdom'.[59] Nonetheless, the war did cause some disruption of pre-war trends. In Londonderry, above all, the unprecedented prosperity which it experienced seems to have reduced intercommunal tensions. More generally, as the war progressed, the border issue receded as a factor in local politics, and 'real' social and economic issues rose to a new level of prominence. This was evidenced in successive by-election defeats for the government and the measurable swing to the left, which so alarmed informed opinion within the unionist movement; Harrisson commented on the strong cross-sectional appeal of the Labour Party. Also Protestants and Catholics did share some vital aspects of wartime experience. Civil defence activities provided increased opportunity for social integration — citizens of both persuasions could serve together as air-raid wardens, rescue workers and fire-fighters. At Easter 1941, after the first heavy raid, the *Irish Times* reported 'the bombs that were hurled on Belfast made no question of religious or political difference. Orangemen and Fenians fell victims alike';[60] afterwards, dazed and bewildered families from both traditions sought to identify the unclaimed bodies brought to St George's market. From all parts of the city, citizens fled in terror from their homes or 'ditched' — huddling during the hours of darkness in some suburban hedgeway, ditch or field. Similar scenes were enacted in cities and larger towns throughout the province; in Londonderry, the authorities feared that as many as 15,000 might cross into Donegal. One of the most enduring of the verifiable folk memories of the war years is of women and children from the Shankill and

Falls gathering in the vaults of Clonard monastery during early May 1941, whilst the Luftwaffe pulverized the streets outside. The Redemptorist priests had opened church property to the local community, whatever their religion, for want of alternative shelter in the area.

But even at the time of the blitz, there were limits to the shared nature of the experience. After the raids, the unclaimed dead were buried in separate graveyards, according to their presumed faith — a potent image in itself of sectarian division. Police reports indicate that in Belfast people preferred to 'ditch' in areas which they knew would attract those predominantly of their own religious persuasion. In Fermanagh, as throughout the province, protestant evacuees billeted with protestant householders and catholic evacuees with catholic householders. Even the geographical distribution of death and destruction caused by the Luftwaffe in Belfast reinforced protestant suspicions that there was collusion between nationalist areas of the city and the enemy, probably via spies operating from the Axis legation in Dublin.[61]

In addition, wartime attitudes seem broadly to have split along traditional sectarian lines. No one could doubt that the Unionist Party supported the war effort. But it was evident to knowledgeable British observers that, even at the level of cabinet minister, the movement lacked the degree of urgency about defeating Hitler found elsewhere in the United Kingdom. Brooke was appalled by 'the general attitude' of the backbenchers; he said of them 'I am afraid no MP realizes there is a war on'. He also recorded that he was 'very angry' with Herbert Dixon, the Chief Whip who 'did not want ration cards' to be introduced into Northern Ireland. In Brooke's opinion: 'if Ulster stands out on this she is doomed. Her loyalty is only skin deep'.[62] A widespread criticism of Andrews was his failure to give clear leadership and to make the war his absolute priority. Spender, therefore, believed that he compared very unfavourably with the example set by Carson in 1914. Overall MacDermott considered that 'there was a certain self-interest about our patriotism in the second world war — there was more in it commercially for Northern Ireland'. The province did show more support for the 1914-18 war than it did in 1939, he believed, but 'one had to remember that, compared with 1914-18, the enthusiasm for the conflict was naturally lower on both sides of the North Channel.'[63] The conclusion reached by Harrisson in his 1942 inquiry was that there were certainly 'many enthusiastic and patriotic citizens, especially among the middle- and upper-class Protestants.' But it was his broad impression that Ulster was 'only helping to fight [the war]. It feels like an active supporter, a yelling spectator' — rather than a part of a country which was itself at war.[64]

In contrast, amongst northern Nationalists there is much evidence of deep-seated hostility or, at least, indifference felt towards the war effort. F.H.

Boland, assistant secretary in the Department of Foreign Affairs in Dublin, stated categorically on 22 April 1941 that 'the vast majority of Nationalists in the six-county area were absolutely pro-German on account of their unjust treatment by the British government and its Belfast puppet'.[65] He was, of course, unlikely to understate the extent of minority alienation. Though attitudes may have varied by locality and class, generally many felt no inclination to fight in or support 'England's war', on behalf of a government whose existence they utterly opposed; this perspective was reinforced by the fact of southern Ireland's neutrality. A local study of Fermanagh, a typical border county, concluded that whilst the unionist population there 'threw themselves wholeheartedly into the war effort', there was 'among some of the catholic community...a certain ambivalence regarding the war. Memories were still very much alive of the troubles of the 1920s, with the war of independence. Many Nationalists felt betrayed by the Westminster government who had promised Home Rule to the whole island at the start of the first world war. A divided country now resulted, with much bitterness felt in the north, by the nationalist community who saw Dublin as their political headquarters'.[66] In 1940, Cahir Healy, a local Nationalist MP, stated 'at all event we [Nationalists] have the consolation that we cannot be much worse off politically than we are'.[67]

Diary records written in Belfast during the war reinforce these impressions from the Ulster border. In July 1940, when allied war prospects seemed bleakest, William McCready, a post office worker in the city, noted of his young catholic fellow employees, 'I believe that they have such a strong dislike or, at least, distrust of Britain that they would as soon trust the Germans and that means Nazi Germany. They look upon the war as being none of their business.'[68] During the following month, Moya Woodside was struck by slogans daubed on gable walls in catholic areas 'Join the IRA,' 'No conscription here', and 'ARP stands for Arrests, Robbery and Police'. She also relayed the experience of a middle-class catholic refugee from Austria who had first settled in Belfast during 1938. 'To mollify the priest' she had agreed (in the spring of 1940) to 'send her child to the neighbouring catholic Sunday school'. Woodside continues: 'The second Sunday, the child came home and said that they had been taught that "Hitler was a good man, who had done so much for his people" and that it would be better for Ireland to have the Germans here than the English. After this her mother naturally took her away.'[69] These sentiments are repeated in Brian Moore's autobiographical *The Emperor of Ice Cream*: the author's father, Mr Burke, a Catholic, remarks with feeling — 'when it comes to grinding down minorities, the German jackboot isn't half as hard as John Bull'.[70]

In Londonderry minority attitudes may have been different, possibly as a result of the ameliorative impact of wartime prosperity and the influence of the Roman Catholic Bishop of Derry, Neil Farren. He strongly opposed conscription but encouraged his congregation to participate in the war effort by, for example, joining the civil defence services. A local study concluded that: 'the contribution of Derry Catholics was as important as that of the city's Protestants and death was no respecter of religious affiliations'. However, it adds that 'the importance of the city to the war effort is not generally recognized locally' and speculated that this may be because 'the nationalist majority population had no wish to remember being such a vital part in Britain's war effort and ... survival'.[71]

Many years later, Brooke alleged that 'one of the Nationalist MPs of the day went so far as writing to the German ambassador [Hempel] in Dublin, asking that if Germany won the war would they unite the two parts of Ireland'.[72] The MP was, in all likelihood, Cahir Healy, though others have disputed Brooke's claim. Nonetheless, when German invasion of Ireland seemed imminent, a report to the Department of Justice in Dublin, supplied by the garda, referred to northern contacts with the legations in Dublin. In August 1940, three Nationalist politicians — Senator McLaughlin from Armagh and John Southwell and Peadar Murney from Newry — 'decided' at a meeting in Dublin, attended by Hempel, 'to place the catholic minority in the north under the protection of the Axis powers'. Soon afterwards, an unnamed Nationalist delegation from Lurgan raised the issue of partition with the German and Italian ministers in Dublin. They both 'promised support' and indicated that the matter would be raised in broadcasts by 'German and Italian controlled radio stations'.[73]

There is also evidence that the two religious communities reacted differently not just to the war itself but to a number of key issues which arose during the course of the conflict. It was the expectation of powerful opposition from the minority to conscription which effectively determined Westminster's decision not to introduce it into Northern Ireland. Cardinal MacRory's statement issued from the Archbishop's Palace, Armagh, on 22 May 1941, makes clear the uncompromising grounds of the church's opposition. It stated that Ireland was 'an ancient land, made one by God. . . partitioned by a foreign power, against the vehement protests of its people. Conscription would now seek to compel those who writhe under this grievous wrong to fight on the side of its perpetrators'.[74] MacRory himself showed little willingness to cooperate with the Northern Ireland government in relation to the war effort and his broad attitude has been described as 'fervently anti-British, if not actually pro-Nazi'.[75] The contrast in community responses could, however, be overstated. It is far from clear that the protestant population in general would have welcomed the introduction of conscription either, though committed Unionists would have done so enthusiastically.

The contrast in attitudes was possibly clearer in relation to civil defence. John Oliver, a leading civil servant in the Ministry of Public Security, noted that it had a greater appeal to Protestants who by 'nature and tradition' were 'organizers and devotees of order and efficiency' and 'identified more fully with the British state'.[76] Catholics were under-represented in the various services; the obligatory oath of allegiance was a potent factor in deterring nationalist recruitment. In west Belfast there was greater hostility directed towards air raid precautions than in other districts. Active antagonism and passive resistance found expression in ARP personnel receiving threatening anonymous letters, being physically attacked and subjected to armed hold-ups. There was a notable shortage of volunteers from the Falls Road. Even before the war (in early June 1939), Republicans held a mass demonstration in the area, which 'ended in a night of violence during which thousands of IRA sympathizers built bonfires out of their government issued gas-masks.'[77]

Religious identity also helped determine local reaction to the United States troops based in Northern Ireland. Tom Harrisson's survey in 1942 concluded that Protestants were 'enthusiastic' in their response; they welcomed the troops for themselves, and for the war effort and 'almost unconsciously as a strengthening of the forces of order against the constant fear of Catholic (nationalist) trouble.'[78] A Ministry of Information official likewise observed in April 1943 that, despite 'a small number of honourable exceptions, . . . [the] . . . welcome given to the Americans had been overwhelmingly on the part of the Unionists and Protestants — those loyal to the British crown and resolved to maintain the British connection.' This he contrasted with the response of the 'Catholic-Nationalist minority'.[79]

Harrisson's enquiry concluded that the catholic population was 'biased towards antagonism' with regard to the American troops, considered their presence 'an insult' and generally suspected that they were 'really there to ensure partition and possibly even to invade the south.' This was of course a broadly accurate perception, especially in 1942. He noted that 'minority propaganda against the Americans has a vigour and viciousness which gives it an advantage in spreading.' It gained credibility from the 'known fact that one of the stories has a basis in truth' — the shooting dead of a bus driver near Londonderry; in the city itself, he noted that 'Catholics tend to dislike or despise' the US forces. He regarded it as an added 'difficulty' that 'large concentrations' of servicemen were stationed in 'strongly catholic areas' like Londonderry or areas along the Antrim coast, which had 'an appreciable undertone of IRA'. He added, however, that 'the bad attitude to [them] is more especially to be found where there are no Americans in the immediate vicinity...their 'conduct and manners' were such that they were difficult to dislike'. Finally he stressed that only a 'minority' within the minority held 'strongly antagonistic views. . . many individual Catholics are thoroughly in favour of [them]'. Overall, Harrisson was convinced that 'a working knowledge of local prejudice is a pre-essential in the maintaining of good relations by any foreign force'.[80]

These views are largely confirmed from other sources — David Gray was particularly concerned that Cardinal MacRory's condemnation of the arrival of the American troops in Northern Ireland would be 'taken as an approval of...the recent IRA manifesto declaring war on the US' and could, by fanning Irish 'resentment', contribute to the murder of American troops in Northern Ireland.[81] Parker Buhrman, the US Consul in Belfast, also highlighted the hostility of local Republicans. In a report (completed in September 1942) he stated that the IRA had denounced the coming of the US troops and thus, soon after the first GIs had arrived, the Falls Road and other nationalist areas of Belfast had been placed off-limits. He continued: 'Individual American soldiers have been subjected to threats by IRA partisans ever since they arrived in the North of Ireland. Quite a number of them have been brutally assaulted under cover of darkness', Londonderry being a particular trouble spot. He reported 'considerable resentment' on the part of the US forces towards the IRA. But it is also evident that Irish-American GIs were often as vehemently anti-British as local Republicans. The senior catholic chaplain with the US forces bluntly told the consul that the 'British should get out of Ireland'.[82]

Conflicting attitudes towards the war fuelled traditional intercommunal rivalry and suspicion. Rev. Dr Bernard Griffin, Archbishop of Westminster, felt justified, on 7 November 1944, in claiming that 'today Roman Catholics are being persecuted in Germany and Poland — and I need hardly mention the persecution that is going on even at the present day in Northern Ireland.' The parallel drawn between the behaviour of the Belfast government and the genocide of the Nazis not surprisingly outraged Brooke and his colleagues. Thus, on 9 November, the Stormont cabinet decided to send a letter of protest to the Home Secretary, Herbert Morrison, pressing him to meet personally the errant archbishop. It stated that the comments which the archbishop had made were 'odious' and tended 'to stir up sectarian trouble from which during the war years we have happily been free'. It asserted that Protestants and Catholics 'have been working together without any sign of sectarian feeling'.[83]

The tone of this statement bore little relation to reality. Employment questions continued to be highly sensitive throughout the war. A recurring theme of the resolutions then (1944-5) being discussed by the Unionist Party's standing committee, for example, was concern at Catholics 'getting in all over the province,' whether purchasing houses or farms or finding employment in the civil service, post office or local industry. It was alleged thay they were exploiting the absence of loyalists who had joined crown forces or migrated to work in English munitions factories.[84] British ministers recognized that some of the reluctance shared by Protestants to leave permanent employment and enlist in crown forces was due to fears that their positions would be taken by someone of the opposite faith (as well as the implicit assumption of substantial long term unemployment after the war). Andrews' view in March 1943, that the appointment of a single, catholic permanent or assistant secretary would 'end the government' indicates the strength of discriminatory forces amongst his supporters.[85]

Moya Woodside had encountered these at first hand. She described two separate cases of boys 'victimized because of their religion', and appearing before a welfare committee on which she served. A government agency had found both 'good jobs' with short hours and 'reasonable' pay, but they had given in their notice after a few days. 'The reason', she writes, was that 'they were Catholics and the boys there, all Protestants, had so intimidated and bullied them that they decided not to go back'. She concluded: 'One can only assume that this sort of bigotry is tacitly approved of by the employers as they do nothing about it'. On another occasion, she had a parallel experience when she sought to find lodging for a.temporarily homeless catholic girl. She telephoned three hostels, including the Salvation Army, 'but all of them, when hearing the girl was a Catholic, found they just hadn't any beds'. She continued: 'One forgets how wide the gulf between Catholic and Protestant is here until something like this happens'.[86]

But Woodside did admit to feelings of prejudice herself. She described interviewing a Belfast woman who 'said she was 28, but looked to be 40 — toothless, haggard, undernourished, thin lank hair ... the mother of eight living children, three of them tubercular, was suspected of TB herself, and her husband of course long-term unemployed Catholic'. She added 'I try not to be intolerant, but a religion which turns women into reproductive machines, regardless of the effect on health and happiness, is brutal and inhumane... There are thousands and thousands like her in this city alone.' In Woodside's opinion, the catholic families were the 'poorest and most unhelpable'.[87] Her anecdotal evidence conformed to a stereotype of the minority, shared by many Protestants. They characterised it as a community whose grievances were not as great as they protested, and largely self-induced — large families lowering living standards, reducing the incentive to work and resulting in a high level of state dependence. With regard to the war effort, they tended to think of northern Nationalists as a sort of fifth column

— pro-German and anti-British by instinct and tradition, ever willing to aid and abet the enemy.

The Stormont Government and the Northern Minority

Given these perspectives, the context of war could itself be used to justify illiberal policies and practices. During its final stages, Spender received representations that houses should be erected 'in certain places on political grounds' (i.e. that houses should be provided for Protestants, in areas which would enhance their electoral strength, irrespective of the applicant's level of need). Though he had in the past forthrightly condemned all discrimination, he considered that there was now 'some justification' for it, because 'Protestants had been more willing to join the forces and volunteer for work in England than Catholics, and are therefore entitled to preferential treatment'. Occasionally, he himself reflected disparagingly on the 'lack of any contribution' made by the minority to the war effort.[88]

However, a more substantial 'contribution' was unlikely to have been encouraged by the suspicion and insensitivity often shown towards the minority by the Stormont government. This was reflected, for example, in the decision to employ leading Unionist Party officials for publicity purposes when attempting to boost military recruitment and, more critically, to use the B Specials as the nucleus of the Local Defence Volunteers. Such policy decisions inevitably reinforced the sectarian image of the security forces in the province. This was in some instances confirmed by their behaviour. In Fermanagh, for example, 'the B Specials did not endear themselves to their catholic neighbours with their officiousness and lack of civility on occasion. Many Catholics were to complain of being stopped at roadblocks by their Home Guard neighbours, Protestants, who asked them their name, address, occupation'.[89] Likewise in Londonderry, there was 'a general feeling' that the smuggled goods seized by B Special patrols 'found its way into the homes of the members'.[90] In contrast, the history of the 53rd division states that it 'adopted a strictly neutral attitude with regard to the two rival factions' and 'gained a well-merited reputation for good behaviour and friendliness and co-operation with all sections of the civil population'.[91] Whatever the accuracy of the claim, such an approach was essential.

Continuing IRA activity, especially during February and April 1940, resulted in increasing numbers of suspects being interned and a high security profile in nationalist areas of Belfast. Woodside was shocked to find the windows in police barracks there 'almost completely bricked up, ... brick structures, apparently for machine guns, built out over the streets ... [and] ... armoured cars with machine guns mounted;' She considered that it was enough 'to withstand a siege' and deduced that full-scale riots must be expected. Even at her bank, outside such districts, she was (in March 1940) 'surprised to see a massive steel railing screwed down to the middle of the counter, which reached within a few feet of the ceiling'.[92]

The most serious IRA incident occurred on 5 April 1942, when constable Patrick Murphy died during an ambush off the Lower Falls Road in west Belfast. The RUC had been intent on preventing any republican commemoration of the 1916 Easter Rising from taking place — Murphy himself was from the neighbouring Beechmount area. Six men were subsequently convicted and sentenced to death, including 22 year old Joe Cahill (who later became IRA Chief of Staff). A protest campaign was organised in sympathy which involved republican organisations, the Northern Ireland Labour Party, the Communist party and some local trade unions; de Valera also intervened to appeal for clemency. Eventually, on Sunday 30 August, all but one prisoner were reprieved. Tom Williams, a 19 year-old from the Clonard area and officer commanding the Belfast Brigade 'C' company, was hanged by executioner Albert Pierpoint at Crumlin Road jail on Wednesday 2 September. He was buried inside the prison, near the hospital wing, his initials scratched on the stonework. Perhaps surprisingly, in view of the spate of republican executions in southern Ireland both during the civil war and World War II, Williams was the first and last in the history of the Northern Ireland state. Sectarian tensions inevitably rose, as the appointed day approached. As a token of sympathy, black flags were flown in west Belfast, and women knelt outside the prison at the time of his execution. Across the street Protestants are alleged to have sung the British national anthem and 'There' ll always be an England'.[93] It was not until July 1945 that the cabinet, somewhat grudgingly, agreed to begin releasing the internees; in Brooke's phrase 'We could not keep them in there for ever'.[94] Throughout their imprisonment, a broad spectrum of nationalist opinion had supported the efforts of the Green Cross Fund to alleviate hardship amongst their families.

Critics of Brooke's leadership argued that, at the outset, he ought to have attempted to heal the province's internal divisions by forming a genuine all-party coalition. Arguably, however, Midgley's inclusion was as far as he could reasonably have gone to make the cabinet more representative. The appointment of a Labour MP as minister, even one so fervently pro-union, caused much unionist criticism and resentment. There would have been far greater political risks involved in incorporating the nationalist members into his government. The IRA threat, the attitude adopted by Cardinal MacRory, and the general indifference of a section of the minority community to the war effort made such cooperation at cabinet level all but inconceivable. As always, the intransigence of one side reinforced that of the other. Many

Unionists regarded cooperation with Nationalists in virtually any sphere of activity as unthinkable. Brooke claimed later 'I knew that I could not invite the Nationalist Party to run in double harness with Unionists. At that time, they were entirely non-cooperative'.[95]

Though some aspects of Northern Ireland government policy were influenced by the narrow prejudices of many of its supporters, it was by no means invariably determined by them. On occasion, ministers led by example and attempted positively to counteract rather than indulge local discriminatory forces. Thus, for instance, the Housing Trust was created in early 1945, partly in response to the rampant discrimination practised by local authorities of whatever political complexion. It had a statutory obligation to provide and allocate working-class houses fairly. Sir Lucius O'Brien, its first chairman, informed the Ulster Unionist Council in May 1950 that there was never any opportunity for undue influence to be used. He explained that allocation was strictly on the basis of an objective points system and also a visit to the applicant's existing accommodation 'to see what kind of housekeepers the women were'. Details of the points system were not published and, though this could have provided scope for discrimination, O'Brien defended it, stating that 'Publication would be dangerous, as it would leave no choice to the Trust in the selection of candidates'.[96] It was, of course, inevitably exposed to powerful political pressures. Nonetheless, analyses of its performance have generally 'exonerated [it] of all conscious desire to discriminate' and concluded that it was a successful and worthwhile initiative.[97] One recent authority writes 'no suggestion was ever made that [it] operated in a sectarian manner'. But he continues 'admittedly the houses it built were of a slightly higher standard than those provided ... by the local authorities and were to this extent less suitable for lower income Catholics'.[98] It selected applicants not strictly on the basis of need, and consequently met the requirements of the majority population more than the minority.

Similarly when the cabinet debated in late 1944 educational reform, Brooke strongly advocated generosity toward catholic controlled schools, advising colleagues that the children must be the 'first consideration'. Hall-Thompson, Corkey's successor as Minister of Education, likewise argued that as catholic pupils comprised about 40% of the school population they 'must be dealt with on a statesmanlike basis', and be accorded 'just treatment'.[99] The resulting legislation, the 1947 Education Act, provided catholic voluntary schools with more generous support from public funds than was then available to comparable institutions in England or had been offered before in Northern Ireland. Patrick Shea was a middle-ranking catholic civil servant in the Ministry of Education during the late 1940s (he was to become one of only two Catholics to reach the rank of permanent secretary in the history of the local civil service). In his opinion the voluntary sector made disproportionately good progress thereafter and his department's reputation for generosity towards the catholic schools was 'well deserved'.[100] Thus the liberal sentiments expressed by ministers in wartime were at least partially translated into practical policy in this case. Nonetheless, the act 'suffered the venom of extreme Protestants while reaping precious little gratitude from the Roman Catholics'.[101]

Likewise in 1945, Stormont ministers decided to introduce family allowances on the same basis as at Westminster, even though it was evident that the minority would benefit disproportionately from the proposed scheme due to its higher birth rate. Ministers regarded its larger average family size with the most acute concern; the introduction of the scheme therefore touched a highly sensitive nerve. Sir Basil recorded a wartime discussion with John McDermott on this issue. Both reached for them the depressing conclusion that there was no immediate 'solution' to the problem of the 'increasing disloyal population'.[102] In fact, though the proportion of Catholics living in the province was rising, it was doing so only slowly. Between 1926-61, it increased from 33.4% to 34.9%, mainly because the minority accounted for approximately 55% of all emigration during these years. Nonetheless these circumstances help account for the acceptance by Stormont ministers of the Beveridge report, their willingness to introduce far-reaching social reforms and commitment to full employment. They had hopes, if not expectations, that these policies might in the long term deflect northern Nationalists from their aspiration to Irish unity. It was Brooke's firm opinion, expressed privately in 1944, that 'the only chance for the political future of Ulster' was if she became 'so prosperous that the traditional political attitudes [were] broken down'.[103] The defect in this approach, which arguably Terence O'Neill continued, was that it entirely neglected the need for structural reform (for example of local government and the security system) and this was a pre-condition of long-term stability in the six counties. Thus, on 15 September 1944, Brooke informed his cabinet that 'after recent discussion with party representatives he was satisfied that there was general acceptance of the view that it would be unwise for the government to provide for the assimilation of the local government and parliamentary franchises'.[104] This decision was myopic; it gave Unionists little advantage and provided the later civil rights movement with its most emotive slogan, 'one man one vote'.

Ministers responded indirectly to the presumed threat posed by the 'growing disloyal population'. They did so by regulating more closely the flow of wartime southern labour coming north to work. Brooke of course appreciated that 'even if we stopped all entry from Eire it would only scratch the difficulty'.[105] A system of residence permits was strictly administered by the Ministry of Home Affairs, under powers derived from the Home Office in London. Much thought was given at Stormont to the possibility of differentiating Eire 'loyalists' (those who favoured partition) from the rest and permitting them to settle permanently in the six counties but it was found impossible to formulate a practicable scheme.

When it seemed that Westminster might not sanction this system of regulation to continue after the war, some ministers favoured the drastic action of having the 1920 Government of Ireland Act amended, so as to provide Stormont with the necessary powers. Dominion status appealed to a number; it would have provided Northern Ireland with roughly the same powers as had been awarded to the south under the terms of the Anglo-Irish Treaty in 1921. Brooke described the whole matter as a 'burning question'.[106] He advised colleagues that unless steps were taken to regulate southern labour coming north in the future, then the protestant ascendancy and the survival of Northern Ireland itself would be placed in jeopardy. Others were equally concerned at the danger of mass unemployment in the north unless action was taken. These considerations became more acute with the extension of social welfare legislation in Northern Ireland post-1945 which, it was feared, would stimulate further cross-border migration. This internal party debate on the merits of constitutional change was given additional impetus by the unexpected course of political events in Britain during the summer of 1945.

The End of War in Sight

Long before then, however, the outcome of the war itself had become entirely predictable. Evidence of the imminence of allied victory was increasingly obvious to alert citizens in Northern Ireland. From early 1943 Belfast's defensive screen was progressively dismantled. During that year, its balloon barrage and anti-aircraft guns, thankfully silent since 1941, were withdrawn (there were no anti-aircraft guns left in the province by 1944), and the air ministry transferred its allocation of night fighters from Aldergrove back to Britain. At the same time, as if to hearten the public, the brickwork constructed to give protection against blast damage around Stormont was removed. On 27 June 1944 Belfast had its last alert; two days earlier the Ministry of Public Security had merged with Home Affairs, in September blackout restrictions were relaxed, and on 31 December the Home Guard was disbanded.

Responding to the changing atmosphere, the *Belfast Telegraph* and the city's corporation organised a Belfast beauty queen contest with readers invited to nominate candidates and submit photographs. It gripped the public imagination: 1,600 responded and 22-year old June Cochrane from Tivoli Gardens was chosen by a panel of judges at a packed Wellington Hall;

hundreds failed to gain admission. In February 1945, as a further step towards normality, parliament recovered the use of the Senate chamber at Stormont — it had been used by the RAF as headquarters from October 1942. Meanwhile, paintings which had been placed in storage when the war started were returned to the City Hall in Belfast.[107]

During the last 12 months of the war, the province was host to three final waves of migrants, affected in contrasting ways by the conflict. The first came involuntarily; on 18 October 1944, Brooke was informed by telephone that '10,000 Boche prisoners may be sent here'. He recorded 'I have written to Morrison, objecting because of the ease of escape ... but told him that if it was urgent, we would accept them'.[108] Two thousand had arrived by mid-January, 1945; the *News Letter* reassured readers that they were 'good Germans', who had 'seen the error of their ways'.[109] Press reports suggested that the reason for their transfer was the 'plentiful supply of food'[110] in rural parts of the province, and because the camps constructed to house allied troops could easily be modified to accommodate them. A further factor mentioned by Maffey to the foreign affairs minister in Dublin was the acute level of overcrowding in south-east England. An obvious cause of concern was that the POWs might escape into Eire and Maffey sought reassurance that, if so, they would be returned by the Irish authorities. By 20 February, 1945, already 20 had broken free, but all were subsequently recaptured; the first couple reached the border on 14 January and, 'after having tea and a chat with the guards', returned 'cheerfully' back to their camp. [111]

Meanwhile, Northern Ireland had become a place of refuge for 7,000 refugees from Gibraltar, who arrived from Great Britain in July 1944, many of them settling near Londonderry. They were fleeing to safety from V1 and V2 flying bomb attacks, then being targeted on London. This new weapon of revenge ('V' stood for revenge) and terror had first been despatched on 12 June, six days after the allied invasion of Normandy. Soon afterwards, the final wave of troops to come to Northern Ireland arrived from Belgium. A total of 25,000 men (4 infantry divisions) came over for training, following the liberation of their country, which was then suffering from acute food shortage and deprivation. They were stationed in various provincial towns, including Armagh, Banbridge and Cookstown. [112]

By the spring of 1945, there was also more tangible evidence of normality returning. Construction work began on houses devastated by German air raids at Greencastle in north Belfast. The area had been one of the first to suffer blitz damage, and was now appropriately the first to benefit from rebuilding. On the night of 16 February 1945, the gaslights in neighbouring streets were turned on. Ten weeks later, on 5 May, air raid precaution members in Belfast were informed by civil defence headquarters on the Lisburn Road that they were being stood down. For several years, their posts had operated mainly as social centres and wardens' duties had largely been confined to stock-taking and writing reports. Three days later, fire-watching regulations were revoked by order in council.

Two Belgian soldiers relax with their Ulster girlfriends at the Giant's Causeway, August 1945
Belfast Telegraph

7
THE END OF WAR:
THE LEGACY

VE Day

Preparing for celebration: flags and bunting being sold off High Street, Belfast (opposite Woolworth's store) on 5 May, 1945
Belfast Telegraph

From late April, 1945, preparations to celebrate the allies' approaching victory had been gathering pace in Northern Ireland. A government announcement specifying which day had been chosen for the festivities was eagerly awaited. The Stormont cabinet had privately agreed to conform with whatever decisions were reached at Westminster. The mood of excitement rose when,

on 2 May, local newspapers reported that both Hitler and Goebbels were dead (they had committed suicide on 30 April). But ominously, the *Northern Whig* headline added *Doenitz — new Fuehrer — says fight goes on.*[1] When news arrived on the evening of Monday, 7 May, that the armistice had been signed, feelings of expectation finally erupted in spontaneous expressions of relief and unconfined jubilation throughout the province. Both communities celebrated, though not necessarily with the same emphasis or intensity. Belfast became, in the words of one reporter, 'a city without strangers'. The *News Letter* stated that 'people from all parts gathered in festive mood'. Along Donegall Place and Royal Avenue, long lines of revellers joined in snake-like procession, dancing in and out of the rows of tramcars immobilised by the crowds. Songs were in the air everywhere. They ranged from 'Tipperary' and the favourites of 1918, to a completely new number composed for the occasion, which began 'Hitler thought he had us with a ya, ya, ya'. For the first time in six years, the sky above the crowded streets glowed with the light of bonfires, bunting festooned thoroughfares, shelters were painted in party colours, drums were beaten and bin-lids clattered. According to one report, 'all the spirit of the Twelfth was there, doubled and redoubled ...it was an opportunity, not only for rejoicing but to stage demonstrations of loyalty to crown and constitution'.[2] Momentously, at one minute after midnight, the conflict in Europe had officially ended.

The carnival atmosphere of VE Day itself (8 May) has left a vivid and lasting impression on the minds of many people then living in Northern Ireland. It was a perfect summer day, a fact which now at last newspapers were at liberty to report. At 3.00 pm, Winston Churchill summarised the absorbing details of German capitulation. In Belfast, his statement was greeted by the ringing of church bells and the celebratory wail of ships' sirens and factory hooters. Many workers were given two days' paid holiday. At Stormont, the House adjourned without transacting any business, so that MPs could join senators in a service of thanksgiving held in the main hall of Parliament Buildings and listen to Churchill's statement on the wireless.

Meanwhile, at the City Hall, the biggest crowd seen there since Covenant Day, 28 September 1912, had assembled. They also listened to the premier's speech, which was broadcast live through loudspeakers. At 10.40 that evening, resounding cheers greeted the switching on of floodlights, which illuminated the building for the first time in almost 6 years. It was by then engulfed by thousands of dancing, cheering, drinking citizens. Total strangers kissed each other, and soldiers were embraced by all and sundry. Bands were improvised, using a variety of instruments — bugles, accordions, drums and, once again, bin-lids. Malcolm Brodie, who had been working on that evening's edition of the *Belfast Telegraph*, joined them; he remembers 'everyone was everybody's friend', it was as though 'you'd been caged up, we'd had no adolescent youth'.[3]

Part of the massive crowd which gathered outside the City Hall, Belfast, to celebrate peace on VE Day, 8 May, 1945
Belfast Telegraph

Elsewhere, away from the city centre, street parties were held. Effigies of Hitler were hung from lampposts. The *News Letter* described, on the Shore Road, 'a bugle band leading a procession of youngsters, in the midst of whom was carried the likeness of Hitler, wearing a swastika, but hanging from gallows'.[4] Thanksgiving services were arranged in churches throughout the city. At one, St. Ninian's in north Belfast, an area twice devastated by the blitz, the congregation was addressed by their minister, the Rev. Finlay Maguire. The caretaker recorded that many of those present had 'used the boiler house as a place of refuge' as no shelters had been built locally. He added that 'the King's speech [at 9 pm] was heard on the wireless at the close'.[5] For many citizens it was a time for reflection. William McCready 'welcomed peace with relief, but could rouse no enthusiasm for the VE Day celebrations. He was absorbed by thoughts of those who had died ... rather than the joy of his many other friends who had survived'.[6]

On a smaller scale, similar scenes of celebration, worship and reflection were reported in other parts of Northern Ireland. In Bangor, one inhabitant remembers an 'explosion of joy', free beer in the public houses and large numbers gathering around the McKee clock at the sea front.[7] In 1939, few at Campbell College, Belfast, could have imagined that they would celebrate the end of hostilities in Europe parading through the streets of Portrush and, after midnight, ending a day of 'mild revelry' on rocks near the shore, burning an effigy of Hitler.[8] The resort had been transformed by the war, with both the Ministry of Education and Stranmillis Teacher Training College evacuated there as well as the school. At Lisburn also, multiple representations of the Fuehrer were consumed by flames — some suspended from a gibbet, others attired as a painter.

Celebrations also away from the City Hall. A street party at Glenwood Street, Shankill Road, Belfast, on VE Day

Belfast Telegraph

In Fermanagh, likewise, houses were decorated, bunting adorned the streets, bonfires were lit in many towns and bases, and effigies burnt. In Newtownbutler 'old political differences were buried for a while, with the coming together of catholic and protestant bands leading a procession of Orangemen ... On the morning of VE Day ... in St Michael's Church in Enniskillen, Solemn High Mass was celebrated to an overflowing congregation in thanksgiving for peace and for the preservation of Ireland from the horrors of war.'[9] At Castle Archdale, convoy escorts and U-boat patrols continued until 3 June. Though the base remained on a war footing, the mood gradually relaxed. Ground crews, who had never been in the air before, eagerly seized the opportunity. Most chose to fly north over the Giant's Causeway, and also Lisahally to see the surrendered U-boats, tied up there before disposal — the face of the enemy with which they were most familiar. When Doenitz had surrendered all German forces to the allies on 4 May, the submarines had been instructed to hand themselves over to the nearest allied ships. Some captains chose to scuttle their boats; others surfaced;

Surrendered German
U-boats tied up at
Lisahally, June 1945
*Public Record Office of
Northern Ireland*

signalled their peaceful intentions and were escorted to port. On 14 May, eight arrived at Lisahally, the first of 43 in total, with Royal Naval guards watching over their skeleton crews which were then taken to a POW camp nearby. One of those already held captive was a German paratrooper, later to become famous as Manchester City's goalkeeper, Bert Trautmann. The cabinet later agreed, after a discussion, to employ some of the prisoners on the grass seed harvest, where no other labour was available.[10]

After The War — An Uncertain Future

In Londonderry itself, popular expressions of delight and celebration over VE Day were somewhat muted, not just because of thoughts of those who had died. It may be that this predominantly nationalist city lacked enthusiasm for celebrating allied victory in what many perceived to be England's war. At any rate, newspaper reports and also those present record a mood of apprehension. There was concern that the end of the war might bring an end not just to the city's cultural diversity but also to its spectacular and unfamiliar affluence. In January 1944, the Town Clerk, in a reply to a request from the Ministry of Information at Stormont, highlighted local peoples' legitimate 'dread of no work for the men after the war'.[11]

Many people throughout Northern Ireland must have been haunted by the spectre of the 'hungry thirties' returning, with prolonged recession, unemployment and poverty. For all the suffering that had occurred, the conflict had brought as well a level of prosperity not known since the first world war. Until May 1945, the most obvious peace dividend had been the withdrawal of troops, the collapse of munitions contracts and the laying off of all civil defence personnel; the return of those who had been enlisted was imminent. Brooke noted privately 'I find I have no feelings of elation, only thankfulness that others will not have to endure the losses that we have suffered. One realises also the vast and difficult problem which lies ahead'.[12] No doubt with these thoughts in mind, the minister consulted his cabinet colleagues, and Glentoran and Andrews, during the euphoria of VE Day and 'decided to go to the country at once'.[13] In due course, on 14 June, an election was held. For the Unionist Party, the results were amongst its worst in the history of Stormont. Though it emerged with 50.4% of the votes cast and 33 seats, this represented a drop of 6% in its share of the poll from the previous contest (9 February 1938) and it had six fewer MPs than before.

Brooke professed to find this outcome totally gratifying: after all his party still held an overall majority of 14 in the new parliament. But it was widely regarded within the movement as a grave setback and a committee was immediately convened to investigate its cause. For the government, its most ominous feature was the stern challenge provided by various labour groups,

German U-boat crew members, Helmut Schmoeckle, Klaus Hilgendorf and Otto Von Faust, having surrendered, are escorted on to the train for Belfast, where they will be interrogated
Imperial War Museum

who had campaigned on social and economic issues. Collectively they had won just five seats, but had attracted the support of 31.9% of those who had voted, compared with 7.4% in 1938.[14] Their efforts had been assisted by defective unionist organisation at constituency level. In Brooke's publicly stated opinion their success was also due to exaggerated fears of future unemployment; privately he fully shared popular concern. In essence it was a measure of the wartime swing to the left in local politics.

Labour Victory at Westminster — the Welfare State

Worse was to come for the unionist leadership. The Stormont result provided local ministers with no premonition regarding the likely outcome of the Westminster elections held in mid-July 1945. The Labour Party's historic victory therefore caused them surprise as well as deep consternation. At a stroke Northern Ireland's principal wartime gain, the real improvement in Westminster-Stormont relations, on which so much depended, seemed in jeopardy. Brooke summarised the reasons for his anxiety — firstly, the new British administration might 'try and create conditions whereby [the north] may be forced into the Free State'; historically the British labour movement had been consistent in its sympathy for the claims of Irish nationalism. Brooke's second concern was that his own government might now be 'compelled to adopt very strong socialist measures'. Either prospect, he believed, could lead to 'complete chaos' and a major constitutional crisis.[15] He and his colleagues therefore pondered the various options open for consideration — preserving things as they were, Irish unity, direct rule from Westminster or, once again, dominion status. With justification, the new Labour Home Secretary, Chuter Ede, characterised the unionist cabinet as 'remnants of the old ascendancy class, very frightened of the Catholics and the general world trend to the left'.[16]

In fact Labour's victory proved to be the prelude to Northern Ireland's best years. The foundations, which had been laid in wartime, were built on by the socialist administration, not demolished. With regard to Ireland, Attlee and his colleagues were as anxious as their predecessors had been to avoid entanglement there. But they were broadly sympathetic in their attitude towards the Stormont leadership. They recognised that a genuine majority in the six counties favoured union with Britain, though they were concerned that the region's electoral procedures fell below the standards of democracy found elsewhere in the United Kingdom. In the longer term, they expected and favoured Irish unification; they were however concerned that north and south should remain within the empire and that the process should be completed gradually and through persuasion, not coercion. Above all they were highly appreciative of the province's wartime role. They compared it favourably with southern neutrality and believed that their feelings of gratitude were widely shared by the British electorate.[17] Douglas Harkness recalled a conversation with a Labour MP, Tom Johnston, after the 1945 Westminster election. Johnston stated 'that the attitude in his party was that Northern Ireland had stood by the United Kingdom during the war in sharp contrast to Eire which had denied the UK the use of ... the ports, ... and that whatever views the Labour Party might have had with regard to the Irish Free State in pre-war years ... the Labour movement would never forget what Northern Ireland had contributed to the United Kingdom war effort and ... would solidly support [it]'. Harkness added, 'later I learnt that the same attitude prevailed with both Attlee and Morrison, who both became firm friends of Ulster'.[18]

The Labour cabinet's collective sense of the strategic importance of Northern Ireland to Britain's security had been transformed by the conflict and helped mould its policy. When talking to Sean MacBride, Irish Foreign Minister, in May 1949, Philip Noel-Baker, Commonwealth Relations Office, stated categorically 'without the help of Northern Ireland, Hitler would undoubtedly have won the submarine war and [we] would have been defeated'. [19] Earlier, in October 1946, Lord Addison, Dominions Office, ventured the opinion that it would be folly in the future to 'throw away that safeguard [i.e. the six counties] unless on terms that will secure its continued availability'.[20]

Throughout its term in office the Labour government treated Northern Ireland more generously than all its predecessors. It honoured fully the financial arrangements which had been reached during inter-governmental negotiations, 1943-4. These formed the basis for two agreements signed in 1946 and 1949, which recognised the province's right and helped fund its efforts to maintain its social services on the same level as elsewhere in the United Kingdom. The Stormont cabinet initiated the necessary reforms with genuine enthusiasm, prompting Herbert Morrison, the Home Secretary, to describe its members as behaving like 'moderate socialists'.[21] Collectively these transformed the face of the north. By 1952, 550,000 workers were covered by a national insurance scheme, roughly 60,000 persons were receiving national assistance and family allowances were being claimed for almost 220,000 children. These measures, combined with the improved performance of the local economy and the setting up of a national health service and tuberculosis authority, contributed to a dramatic fall in the regional death rate. In 1939, it was the highest in the United Kingdom; by 1962 it was lower than any area in Great Britain. Meanwhile the first significant steps since partition were taken in response to the province's acute housing shortage and the 1947 Education Act made secondary education free and compulsory for all.

These major post-war social reforms (heavily funded by the imperial exchequer) helped open a gap in living standards between northern and southern Ireland. At the same time, despite claims of unfairness regarding their implementation, they helped provide a framework for Northern Ireland's internal stability. At least in the short term they generated encouraging signs of social integration, reconciliation and increased tolerance, during the fifties and early sixties. Unionist publicity by the late forties was already more confident and aggressive. In 1949, a UUC publication was cumbersomely entitled *Warning to the Ulster people, keep Ulster British, it's your money Eire is after; how an all-Ireland republic would affect your social services*. On 8 December 1947, the *Belfast Telegraph*, in similar vein, carried a leading report on 'Ulster's success and Eire's failure.' Three weeks earlier, a northern minister, Edmund Warnock, claimed in an article in *The Times* that the level of living standards in north and south was so 'dissimilar as to be scarcely comparable'. De Valera was stung into making a reply in the Dail on 26th November.[22] He found Warnock's statistical analysis difficult to refute but urged that if the Stormont cabinet was so convinced of the superior quality of life in the six counties it should hold a plebiscite on Irish unity in, for example, Fermanagh and Tyrone. But some of Brooke's colleagues were convinced that political progress was also being made. In August 1951, Brian Maginess claimed 'the number of Catholics who are gradually coming to have faith in us, our permanent constitutional position and our fair administration would appear to be increasing considerably'.[23]

Maginess's reference to 'our permanent constitutional position' related back to events in 1948-9. The Labour Party's changed assessment of the province's strategic importance to Britain, which had resulted from the war, had then found tangible expression in the 'declaratory' clause of the Ireland Act, 1949. It had passed this measure in response to Eire's decision to sever its last links with the commonwealth and become the fully independent 'Republic of Ireland.' Whilst its terms were being discussed, the Stormont leadership requested that it should include a clause clearly stating that Northern Ireland would remain as part of the United Kingdom for as long as a majority at Stormont wished. Though its inclusion is usually regarded as one of Brooke's foremost achievements, in fact Attlee had readily accepted the proposal. He did so partly because he believed that it would be genuinely popular with the British electorate, now more sympathetic to Ulster's claims because of its wartime role. Also, he was firmly convinced that it was in Britain's immediate and vital interests. His cabinet was sternly advised in a report, dated 5 January 1949, written by leading Whitehall officials, that 'it has become a matter of first class strategic significance for this country, that the north should continue to form part of His Majesty's dominions. So far as can be foreseen, it will never be to Great Britain's advantage that Northern Ireland should form part of a territory outside His Majesty's jurisdiction. Indeed it seems unlikely that Great Britain would ever be able to agree to this, even if the people of Northern Ireland desired it'.[24] The north's wartime role, combined with Eire's new status, had clearly made a profound impact on the British establishment's calculations, especially given the context of the cold war.

The Second World War was a significant milestone in Northern Ireland's history chiefly because it resulted in much warmer relations between Westminster and Stormont. This was the key to the transformation in its social welfare services which occurred during the post-war decades. It also provided Unionists with greater constitutional security. On several occasions, however, Attlee had reminded Brooke that the British parliament was sovereign, that it could not bind its successors and that thus a subsequent parliament might well repeal or revoke the declaratory clause. During the '50s and early '60s, the province was stable but remained deeply divided. North-South relations had, by contrast, shown least change. In wartime the gulf had widened further and this process continued apace, when Eire became an independent republic on 8 April 1949. The change in its status raised nationalist excitement throughout the island, and resulted in a virulent anti-partition campaign, lasting over several years; unity seemed the logical next step, the only unfinished business. Sir John Maffey, now Lord Rugby, British ambassador in Dublin, feared that this rising tide of emotion might bring the gun back into Irish political life and cause a grave state of disorder in Ulster. He offered what might now, with the benefit of hindsight, be seen as prophetic advice to those Unionists who felt that the forces of the Crown would soon 'teach them [the gunmen] a lesson'. He warned; 'It will be a day of triumph for Eire if the forces of the Crown are actively employed against patriotic elements in Ireland. British bayonets are Ireland's secret weapon'.[25]

Sir Basil Brooke, then Northern Ireland's Prime Minister, speaking to wounded soldiers after a Victory Day parade on Sunday, 13 May 1945
Belfast Telegraph

NOTES

INTRODUCTION

1   Breege McCusker, *Castle Archdale and Fermanagh in World War II* (Irvinestown, 1993), pp 2, 8.
2   John Bowman, *De Valera and the Ulster Question, 1917-73* (Oxford 1982), p 311.
3   Norman Brook to Clement Attlee, 5 January 1949, in Public Record Office, Kew (henceforth PRO) Premier 8/1464.

CHAPTER 1

1   *Parliamentary Debates (Commons), XXIII* 4 September 1939, col. 1902.
2   *Ibid., XXI,* 22 March 1938, col. 328.
3   Diary of Moya Woodside, 24 February 1941 and *passim*, MO5462, Tom Harrisson Mass Observation Archive, University of Sussex. (Henceforth *Woodside Diary*).
4   *Ibid.,* 12 March 1940.
5   *Ibid.,* 26 October 1940.
6   *Ibid.,* 29 December 1940.
7   Peadar Livingstone, *The Fermanagh Story* (Enniskillen, 1969), p 340.
8   McCusker, *op.cit.,* p 12.
9   *Ibid.,* p 25.
10 *Woodside Diary,* 29 August, 9 November 1940.
11 *Ibid.,* 8 December 1940, 11 January 1941, 18 August 1941.
12 *Ibid.,* 7 March 1940.
13 Richard Doherty, *Key to Victory; The Maiden City in the Second World War* (Antrim, 1995), p 56.
14 Douglas Harkness 'But I Remember', unpublished autobiography, p.127, in Harkness Papers, Public Record Office of Northern Ireland (henceforth Harkness, PRONI).
15 McCusker, *op.cit.,* p14.
16 Garda Report, 10 November 1941, in D/FA, P 305/1, National Archives, Dublin (henceforth NAD).
17 McCusker, *op.cit.,* p102.
18 Garda Report, 8 August 1941 in NAD D/FA P 305/1 *op.cit.*

19 *Ibid.,* Garda Report, 11 September 1941.
20 Reports in Inspector General's Office, Folder No 56, 1945, in PRONI, CAB 3A/78.
21 Report dated 30 April 1942 in NAD D/FA P 305/1 *op.cit.*
22 Dulanty to Department of Foreign Affairs, 19 November 1941, in NAD, D/FA P 305/1 *op.cit.*
23 *Ibid.,* report by J. Kenny, 12 May 1941.
24 *Ibid.,* Garda Report, 7 December 1944.
25 *Sunday News,* 23 January 1968.
26 Harkness, *op.cit.,* p 122.
27 *Woodside diary,* 16 September 1940, 31 January, 30 August 1941.
28 Report by Harold Wilson, dated 2 January 1941, in PRONI, COM 61/440.
29 Financial diary of Sir Wilfrid Spender, 16 December 1940, in PRONI, D715 (henceforth *Fin Diary*)
30 *Sunday Pictorial,* 4 April 1943
31 Mass Observation Archive, *op.cit.,* FR 1309, dated 12 June 1942.
32 *Irish Independent,* 13 May 1939.
33 De Valera's views, summarized in Dulanty to Chamberlain, 26 April 1939, NAD D/FA P 70.
34 Diary of Lady Craigavon, 2 May 1939 in PRONI, D1415/B/38.
35 *Fermanagh Times,* 11 May 1939.
36 Margery Boyd, *War Record, Queen's University, Belfast* (Belfast, 1948), *passim* and Keith Haynes, *Neither Rogues Nor Fools; A History of Campbell College and Campbellians* (Belfast, 1993), *passim.*
37 *Fermanagh Times,* 13 July 1933.
38 *Brooke Diary,* 1, 2 July 1940 in PRONI, D3004/D (hereafter *Brooke Diary*).
39 B. Barton, *The Blitz: Belfast in the War Years* (Belfast, 1989), p 50.
40 *Woodside Diary,* 7 October 1940.

41 Bevin to Churchill, 13 April 1943, PRO, CAB 123/92.

42 *Fin Diary*, 26 December 1940, 4 January 1941.

43 Smiles to Shuster, 4 December 1942, in PRONI, COM 61/939.

44 Scott to Wickham, 13 April 1942, in PRONI COM 61/939.

45 Robert Fisk, *In Time of War; Ireland, Ulster and the Price of Neutrality, 1939-45* (London, 1983), p 413.

46 *Woodside Diary*, 27 February 1940.

47 James Doherty, *Post 381: The Memoirs of a Belfast Air Raid Warden* (Belfast 1989), pp 6, 8.

48 *Woodside Diary*, 21 December 1940.

49 Barton, *The Blitz*, *op.cit.*, p 79.

50 Report on visit to Belfast on 16-17 April 1941 by Major Sean O'Sullivan, in NAD, D/T S 14993.

CHAPTER 2

1 Mass Observation Archive, *op.cit.*, FR 1309.

2 PRONI, CAB 4/473, 15 May 1941; also John Blake *Northern Ireland in the Second World War* (Belfast, 1956), p 368.

3 Mass Observation Archive, FR 1309.

4 *Ibid.*

5 *Fin Diary*, *op.cit.*, 2 August 1938.

6 Blake, *op.cit.*, p 191.

7 *Parl. Deb. (c)*, XXIII, 25 September 1940, cols. 2155, 2161, 2171.

8 *Ibid.*, XXIII, 19 June 1940, cols. 1505, 1506.

9 P. Buckland, *The Factory of Grievances: Devolved Government in Northern Ireland, 1921-39* (Dublin, 1979), p 1.

10 B. Barton, *Brookeborough; the Making of a Prime Minister* (Belfast 1988) pp 131-151 *passim*; Woodside Diary, 30 August 1940.

11 Blake, *op.cit.*, pp 168 and 166-171 *passim*; Barton, *The Blitz*, *op.cit.*,. pp 58-79.

12 Mass Observation Archive, FR 1309.

13 *Woodside Diary*, 27 August, 14 October, 30 November 1940, 22 January 1941; Blake, op.cit., p 83.

14 *Ibid.*, p 171.

15 Mass Observation Archive, FR 1309.

16 IRA Special Communique, dated 10 September 1941, in MS 22309, JJ O'Connell Papers, National Library of Ireland (henceforth NLI.).

17 Quoted in *Woodside Diary*, 23 July 1941.

18 *Ibid.*, 23 July 1941.

19 Harkness, *op.cit.*, p 197.

20 Speech contained in NAD, D/T S10784A.

21 Mass Observation Archive, FR 1309.

22 Fisk, *op.cit.,* p 87.

23 C.N. Barclay, *The History of the 53rd (Welsh) Division in the Second World War* (London, 1956), p 33.

24 *Woodside Diary*, 20 October 1940.

25 Fisk, *op.cit.*, p 231.

26 A. Maxwell to N. Brook, 13 February 1941 in PRO, CAB 123/197.

27 *Ibid.*, Morrison to Margesson, 1 December 1940.

28 *Ibid.*, Margesson to Morrison, 15 January 1941.

29 *Ibid.*, Morton to Allen, 8 February 1941.

30 *Parl. Deb (c), XXIV*, 27 March 1941, col 597; Cabinet Conclusions, 25 March 1941, PRONI, CAB 4/467; PRO, CAB 123/197, Anderson to Churchill, 28 March 1941.

31 Fisk, *op.cit.*, p 233; Blake, *op.cit.*, pp 80-82.

32 Review of IRA activity, 1932-45, in NAD, D/T S11564A.

33 Nigel West, *MI5; British Security Service Operations, 1909-1945* (London, 1981), p 305; also pp 309-328 *passim*.

34 *Sunday Times*, 6 July 1969, According to this Report the Irishman responsible was never captured; see also NAD D/FA S113(a) *passim*.

35 Dermot Keogh, *Twentieth Century Ireland, Nation and State* (Dublin, 1994) p 113.

36 Martin Gilbert, *Finest Hour; W.S. Churchill, 1939-41* (London, 1983) p 432.

37 Minute by Joseph Walshe, 24 May 1940, in NAD, D/FA A3.

38 Record of IRA action in Ireland, 1939-50, note dated 9 October 1946, in NAD, D/T S11564A.

39 *Brooke Diary*, 5 June 1940.

40 Broadcast by Churchill on eve of Battle of Britain, 18 June 1940.

41 *Fin Diary*, 25 May 1940; *Brooke Diary,* 22 May 1940.

42 Interview with John Brooke, 23 February 1985; Fisk, *op.cit.*, pp 185-6.

43 Unsigned memorandum, 1 July 1940, in NAD, D/FA P 13.

44 Craig to Chamberlain, 27 June 1940, in PRO, Premier 3/131/2.

45 *Ibid.*, Chamberlain to Craig, probably 28 June 1940 (undated).

46 *Ibid.*, Craig to Chamberlain, 29 June 1940.

47 Quoted in UUC publication, *Eire and the War, De Valera's Anti-British Record* (Belfast, 1946).

48 MacDonald to Churchill, 28 June 1940, in PRO, Premier 3/131/2.

49 Undated note by Walshe, to de Valera, in NAD, D/FA A2. He also observed 'the pope thinks we should stay neutral'.

50 Denis Parsons, 'Mobilization and Expansion, 1939-40', in *The Irish Sword*, XIX, p 18.

51 Note by Churchill, 18 June 1940, in PRO Premier 4/53/2.

52 Statement by de Valera in Dail, 19 April 1950, in NAD, D/T S 14782A.

53 *Ibid*, NAD, S 14782A.

54 *Ibid*, NAD, S14782A, note dated 4 May 1950, by Ambassador to Holy See.

55 Paul Canning, *British Policy towards Ireland, 1921-41* (Oxford, 1985), pp 313-4.

56 Speech in NAD, D/T S 14782A, *op.cit.*

57 Report by Walshe, NAD, D/FA A2, dated 22 April '41.

58 Speech dated 25 March 1944, in NAD, D/FA A53.

59 Record of conversation dated 23 April 1941, in NAD, D/FA S203. Menzies considered the neutrality policy to be incomprehensible, as he believed 'the saving of civilization' to be the issue at stake in the Second World War.

CHAPTER 3

1 Lady Craigavon diary, 24 November 1940, in PRONI, D1415/B/38.

2 *Fin Diary*, 26-27 November 1940.

3 Interview with Sir Arthur Kelly, 21, 28 April 1979.

4 *Brooke Diary*, 27 November 1940.

5 Report dated 1 January 1941, in PRO, FO 371/29108. Shaw had been a Southern Irish Unionist, assistant secretary to the Irish Convention and secretary to Lord French when Lord Lieutenant of Ireland.

6 *Woodside Diary*, 26 February 1941.

7 Barton, *The Blitz, op.cit.*, p 72.

8 Blake, *op.cit.*, p 168.

9 Barton, *The Blitz, op.cit.*, p 65.

10 Report by O'Sullivan, *op.cit.*, in NAD, S14993.

11 Emma Duffin Diary, pp 86-111, in PRONI, D2109/13.

12 Blake, op.cit., p 233

13 In note by Walshe, 21 April 1941, NAD, D/FA A2.

14 *Ibid.*, note by Walshe, 17 April 1941.

15 Duffin Diary, *op.cit.*, D2109/13.

16 Barton, *The Blitz, op.cit.*, p 168.

17 Report by O'Sullivan, *op.cit.*, in NAD, S 14993.

18 *Woodside Diary*, 17, 18 April 1941.

19 *Ibid.*, 17, 18 April 1941.

20 McCusker, *op.cit.*, p 139

21 *Woodside Diary*, 16, 25 July, 7 August 1941.

22 *The War Years, Derry 1939-'45* (Derry, 1992), p 50

23 *Ibid.*, p 35.

24 Cabinet Conclusions, 15 May 1941, PRONI, CAB 4/473.

25 O. Henderson to R. Gransden, 13 May 1941, in PRONI, CAB 9CD/217.

26 See PRO, CAB 65/52, 53 in 22 and 26 May 1941.

27 *Woodside Diary*, 21 May '41.

28 PRO, CAB 65/49, 12 May 1941.

29 De Valera to Churchill, 25 May 1941, in NAD, D/FA P 70.

30 *Ibid.*, Record of Churchill conversation with Dulanty, 22 May 1941.

31 Eunan O'Halpin, 'Aspects of Intelligence', in *The Irish Sword*, XIX,

p 64; also PRO, CAB65/52, 53 on 22 and 26 May 1941.

32 *Ibid.*

33 Note by Dulanty, 21 May 1941, in NAD, D/FA P 70.

34 PRO, CAB 65/53, on 26 May 1941.

35 PRO, CAB 65/54, on 27 May 1941.

36 *Brooke Diary*, 20 March 1942.

37 *Woodside Diary*, 28 May 1941.

38 Graham Walker, *The Politics of Frustration: Harry Midgley and the Failure of Labour in Northern Ireland* (Manchester, 1985), p 123.

39 *Ibid.*, p 126.

40 *Ibid.*, p 128, 129.

41 *Ibid.*, p 129

42 *Fin Diary*, 23 November 1942.

43 J. Budge and C. O'Leary, *Belfast: Approach to Crisis; A Study in Belfast Politics, 1613-1970* (London, 1973), pp 153, 156.

44 Cabinet Conclusions, PRONI, CAB 4/505, on 20 April 1942.

45 *Ibid.*, PRONI, CAB 4/512, on 8 June 1942.

46 Budge and O'Leary, *op.cit.*, pp 154, 155.

47 MacDermott to Andrews, 2 November 1942, in PRONI, CAB 9CD/22/1.

48 *Ibid.*, Kemp to Andrews, 22 September 1941.

49 *Ibid.*, Churchill to Andrews, 15 October 1942.

50 *Fin Diary*, 27 October 1942.

51 Ormeau Unionist Association to Andrews, 26 October 1942, in PRONI, CAB 9CD/22/1.

52 *Ibid.*, MacDermott to Andrews, 2 November 1942.

53 Churchill to Roosevelt, 11 April 1943, in PRO, CAB 66/36.

54 Andrews to Gordon, 4 November 1942, in PRONI, CAB 9C/22/1.

55 *Fin Diary*, 10, 16 December 1941.

56 John Oliver, *Working at Stormont* (Dublin, 1978), p 68.

57 *Belfast News Letter*, 3 June 1941.

58 John Ditch, *Social Policy in Northern Ireland between 1939-50* (Avebury, 1988) p 83.

59 Patrick Shea, *Voices and the Sound of Drums,* (Belfast, 1981), p 57.

60 Mass Observation Archive, *op.cit.*, FR 2101, dated 20 May 1944.

61 *Fin Diary*, 6 June 1942, PRONI, CAB 4/510, 513 on 2 and 19 June 1942.

62 Note by Sir Horace Wilson, 4 August 1942 in PRO, T160/1327/32563.

63 *Ibid.*, comments by Brooks, 31 July, Gilbert, 11 August and Brittain, 5 August 1942.

64 Wood to Andrews in *Fin Diary*, 14 and 24 September 1942.

65 *Ibid.*, 19, 24 September 1942.

66 Walker, *op.cit.*, p 147

67 *Brooke Diary*, 10 September 1942.

68 *Parl. Deb. (C).*, XXV, 30 July 1942, cols 2456, 2485-2494, 2499-2504.

69 'I.A.N.' to Osbert Peake, 6 May 1941 in PRO, HO 45/20268.

70 B. Barton, *Brookeborough; the Making of a Prime Minister* (Belfast, 1988) p 184 and *passim.*

71 Walker, *op.cit.*, p 129.

72 Cabinet Conclusions, PRONI, CAB 4/473, 15 May '41.

73 *Fin Diary*, 18 January 1943.

74 *Belfast News Letter*, 12 January 1943.

75 *Brooke Diary*, 11, 12 January 1943

76 *Belfast News Letter*, 16 January 1943.

77 Minutes of Meetings of Ulster Unionist Parliamentary Party, 19 January 1943, in Ulster Unionist Party Papers PRONI, D1327/10/1.

78 *Fin Diary*, 20 January, 24 February 1943.

79 Minutes of Parliamentary Party, *op.cit.*, 19 March 1943, PRONI, D1327/10/1.

80 *Brooke Diary*, 25 March, 16 April 1943.

81 *Ibid.*, 21 April 1943.

82 Minutes of Parliamentary Party, 28 April 1943, in PRONI, D1327/10/1.

83 *Belfast News Letter*, 29 April 1943.

84 Andrews to Churchill, 30 April 1943, in PRO, Premier 4/53/1.

85 *Fin Diary*, 28 June 1941, 23 January and 3 March 1943.

86 *Brooke Diary*, 16, 20 January '43.

CHAPTER 4

1 *Fermanagh Times*, 13 July 1933.

2 *Sunday News*, 14 January 1968.

3   Brooke Memoirs, unpublished, in PRONI, D3004/D/46.

4   Interview with John MacDermott, 14 May 1979.

5   *Brooke Diary*, 26 March 1943.

6   Mass Observation Archive, *op.cit.*, FR2101.

7   *Fin Diary*, 12 May 1943.

8   Walker, *op.cit.*, pp 149

9   *Ibid.*, p 150.

10   Cabinet Conclusions, PRONI, CAB 4/541, 6 May 1943.

11   Minutes of Annual Meeting of Ulster Unionist Council, 2 March 1944 in PRONI, D1327/8/10.

12   *Brooke Diary*, 10 October 1943.

13   *Ibid.*, 25 March 1943.

14   *Ibid.*, 19 July 1944; Ulster Unionist Council Papers PRONI, D1327, *passim*.

15   *Brooke Diary*, 23 March 1945.

16   *Fin Diary*, 12 and 25 February 1944; *Brooke Diary*, 8, 11th, 17 February 1944.

17   *Brooke Diary*, 19 April 1945; Minutes of Parliamentary Unionist Party, 19 September, 10 October 1944 and 2 May 1945 in PRONI, D1327/22; Cabinet Conclusions, 15 September 1944 and 19 April 1945 in PRONI, CAB4/597, 622.

18   B. Barton, *The Blitz*, pp 156, 157.

19   'Report to the Special Committee of Belfast Corporation on the Muncipal Health Services of the City', dated 24 December 1941, by Dr Thomas Carnwath, Henry Collection, Queen's University, Belfast.

20   Cabinet Conclusions, PRONI, CAB 4/595.

21   *Fin Diary*, 27 September 1943.

22   Walker, *op.cit.*, p 163.

23   Cabinet Conclusions, 6 May 1943 in PRONI, CAB 4/541.

24   *Belfast Newsletter*, 2 December 1942.

25   Spender to E. Clark, *Fin Diary*, 4 August 1943.

26   *Brooke Diary*, 2 May 1944; Walker, *op.cit.*, pp 155, 156.

27   Cabinet Conclusions, 6 February 1945, in PRONI, CAB 4/614.

28   *Woodside Diary*, 12 October 1941.

29   Cabinet Conclusions, 19 April 1945, PRONI, CAB 4/622.

30   *Brooke Diary*, 4, 8 April 1941, also 24, 27 May 1941.

31   PRO, CAB 65/54, 17 May 1941.

32   Cabinet Conclusions, 19 April 1945, PRONI, CAB 4/622.

33   *Woodside Diary*, 25 May 1941.

34   Minute by H. Morrison, 29 October 1946, in PRO, HO 45/24213.

35   *Ibid.*

36   *Ibid.*, note by Charles Markbreiter, 9 May 1945.

CHAPTER 5

1   Note by J. Walshe, 17 April 1941, in NAD, D/FA A2.

2   *Volkischer Beobachter*, 6 May 1941.

3   Fisk, *op.cit.*, p 408.

4   *Brooke Diary*, 24 July 1945. For Northern Ireland's economic role in the war see also Parl. Deb. (C), 24 July 1945, cols. 71-74; Barton, *Brookeborough op.cit.*, pp 171-190; Blake, *op.cit.*, pp 367-418; K.S. Isles and N Cuthbert, *An Economic Survey of Northern Ireland* (Belfast, 1957); *Ulster Year Books* (Belfast, 1924, 1929 and 1953); L. Kennedy, *The Modernization of Ireland 1940-88* (Dublin, 1988).

5   W D Flackes, *The Enduring Premier* (Belfast, 1962).

6   Blake, *op.cit.*, p 410.

7   Brooke Diary, 31 December 1942.

8   Michael Moss and John R. Hume, *Shipbuilders to the World: 125 Years of Harland and Wolff* (Belfast 1986), p 301; N.L. Middlemas, *British Shipbuilding Yards,* Vol. III (London 1992), p 61.

9   Malcolm Brodie, *The Tele: A History of the Belfast Telegraph* (Belfast, 1995) pp 71-2.

10   *Woodside Diary*, 24 August 1940.

11   Blake, *op.cit.*, pp 200, also 194-200 *passim*.

12   David Fraser, *Alanbrooke* (London, 1982), p 38.

13   Blake, *op.cit.*, p 488.

14   Interview with James Molyneaux, 20 March 1995; Ann Purdie, *Molyneaux,*

15 *Belfast News Letter*, 10 May 1945.

16 File on 'Leading Seaman J J Magennis V.C.', Box 32, Imperial War Museum, London.

17 Blake, *op.cit.*, pp 534-5; *Royal Air Force in Northern Ireland, Official V.E. Day Fiftieth Anniversary Souvenir Brochure* (Belfast, 1995), *passim*.

18 *The Times*, 6 May 1938.

19 *The Irish Times*, 8 November 1938.

20 D. Keogh, *Ireland and Europe, 1919-1989* (Cork, 1989) pp 163-4.

21 In report by Dulanty to Department of Foreign Affairs, 22 May 1941, in NAD, D/FA P 70.

22 *The Times*, 7 November 1940.

23 Doherty, *op.cit.*, p vi.

24 NAD, D/FA A3, *passim*.

25 *Belfast News Letter*, 12 July 1943.

26 Churchill to Andrews, 6 May 1943, PRO, Premier 4/53/1.

27 Fisk, *op.cit.*, p 193.

28 Churchill to General Ismay, 31 May 1940, Churchill Papers, Churchill College Archives, Cambridge, 20/13.

29 Fisk, *op.cit.*, pp. 226-7; Blake, *op.cit.*, pp 154-5.

30 Peter Young, 'Defence and the new Irish State', pp 1-17 and Donal O'Carroll 'The Emergency Army' in *The Irish Sword, XIX*, pp 19-46.

31 *Civilian War Duties* (Dublin 1939). Public Information Pamphlet, No. 1, issued by the Department of Defence.

32 Colm Mangan 'Plans and Operations' in *The Irish Sword, XIX*, p 47.

33 Barclay, *op.cit.*, pp 35, 36.

34 Comment by de Valera at inter-governmental meeting for the Coordination of Defence, 2 August 1940, in NAD, D/FA A3.

35 Barclay, *op.cit.*, p 34.

36 Keogh, *Twentieth Century Ireland*, *op.cit.*, p117.

37 *Ibid.*, p 117.

38 Colm Mangan, 'Plans and Operations', *op.cit.*, pp 47-56.

39 Note dated 17 February 1941, in NAD, D/FA A3.

40 Barclay, *op.cit.*, pp 33, 41 and *passim*.

41 *Ibid.*, pp 38-9; Blake, *op.cit.*, pp 153-169.

42 Barclay, *op.cit.*, pp 34, 36, 37.

43 *Woodside Diary*, 12 October 1940.

44 Tony Canavan, *Frontier Town: Newry, an Illustrated History* (Belfast, 1989), p 209.

45 Blake, *op.cit.*, p 367.

46 *Ibid.*, pp 367-369, Chapter 8, *passim*.

47 David Reynolds, *Rich Relations: The American Occupation of Britain, 1942-45* (London, 1995), p 14.

48 Memorandum by Churchill, 16 December 1941, Churchill Papers 4/235; also telegram by Churchill, 18 October 1941, 20/44, Churchill Papers.

49 Note by Lord Halifax, 23 December 1941, PRO, Premier 3/458/7.

50 *Brooke Diary*, 7 January 1942.

51 'Notes from Lieutenant Colonel Leonard Webster's Typescript' in PRONI, FIN 17/2/19; Blake, *op.cit.*, Chapter 7, *passim*.

52 Reynolds, *op.cit.*, p 243

53 Notes by Leonard Webster, *op.cit.*, PRONI, FIN 17/2/19.

54 NAD, D/FA P 43/1, 2, 3 *passim*.

55 Reynolds, *op.cit.*, pp 118, 119. Blake, *op.cit.*, p 271

56 Reynolds, *op.cit.*, pp 118, 119.

57 McCusker, *op.cit.*, p 26

58 Langford Lodge Wartime Centre, Langford Lodge, Co Antrim.

59 In *Colliers*, (US national weekly publication), 1 January 1944.

60 J. Mullen and D. Francis, 'Base One Londonderry' in *Ulster Folklife*, vol. 41, 1995, p 14.

61 Garda report, dated 7 Febuary 1942, in NAD, D/FA P 43/1.

62 Doherty, *op.cit.*, pp 20-27; Blake, *op.cit.*, Chapt. 7; interview with Charlie Gallagher, Londonderry, 3 July 1988.

63 Garda report, 22 April 1942, in NAD, D/FA P43/1.

64 Mass Observation Archive, *op.cit.*, FR 1306, 8 June 1942.

65 Notes by Webster, *op.cit.*, PRONI, FIN 17/2/19.

66 Mass Observation Archive, FR 1306, *op.cit.*

67 *Ibid.*

68 Doherty, *op.cit.*, p 51.

69 Graham Smith, *When Jim Crow met John Bull* (London, 1987), p 140

70 Reynolds, *op.cit.*, p 228; D. Parker to R. Gransden, 3 January 1944, in PRONI, CAB 9CD/225/19.

71 *Ibid.*

72 Smith, *op.cit.*, p 140.

73 *Ibid.*, p 140.

74 *Ibid.*, p 198.

75 *Brooke Diary*, 2 September 1942.

76 Reynolds, *op.cit.* p 221.

77 Mass Observation Archive, FR 1306, *op.cit.*

78 McCusker, *op.cit.*, p 131.

79 Brodie, *op.cit.*, pp 87, 92; Notes by Webster, *op.cit.*, PRONI, FIN 17/2/19.

80 Reynolds, *op.cit.*, p 258.

81 *Eire and the War, Mr de Valera's Anti-British Record, op.cit.*; *Belfast Telegraph*, 25 August 1945.

CHAPTER 6

1 Fisk, *op.cit.*, p 470.

2 *Parl. Deb. (C)*, XXIX, 18 July 1945, cols. 11, 12.

3 *Ibid.*, I, 23 June '21, cols. 19-22.

4 *Belfast News Letter*, 1 October 1945, see also Dalton's speech in *Belfast News Letter*, 15 September 1945 re 'brave little Northern Ireland, who gave us what other countries refused in the dark hours'.

5 Churchill to Andrews, 6 May 1943 in PRO, Premier 4/53/1.

6 *Belfast News Letter*, 13 June 1945; *Brooke Diary*, 12 June 1945.

7 Keogh, *Twentieth Century Ireland*, *op.cit.*, p 114.

8 Note, dated 12 August 1940, in NAD, D/FA P 51.

9 NAD, D/T S 15262, *passim*; NAD, D/FA A3, *passim*; Keogh *Twentieth Century Ireland, op.cit.*, pp 120-125; TCC/LL/1085, No 21 Imperial War Museum.

10 NAD, D/FA P 43/1, 2, 3, *passim*.

11 IRA Manifesto, 29 August 1942, in NAD, D/T S 11564A.

12 Gray to Cardinal MacRory, 7 October 1942, in Hayes Papers, NLI, Ms 22984; also see note on Maffey's views, 19 February 1941, in NAD, D/FA 5203, NAD, D/FA P 43/1, 2, 3 *passim*. Ireland refused entry to British troops partly because of the 'political situation' in Eire, and suspicions that Britain was exploiting the crisis to re-occupy Ireland - see Walshe to de Valera, 15 July 1940, NAD, D/FA A2.

13 Note, dated 21 February 1944, in NAD, D/FA A53, from U.S. to Dublin government.

14 J.T. Carroll, *Ireland in the War Years, 1939-45* (Newton Abbot, 1975), p 146.

15 Comment by J. Dillon, in *Dail Eireann*, vol. 97, No. 9 col. 2603.

16 See cuttings in NAD, D/FA P98.

17 Dulanty's record of talks with Churchill on 22 May 1941 in NAD, D/FA P 70. See also Dulanty's comments, on 26 May 1941, in NAD, D/T S 203. He refers to the 'depth and bitterness' of Churchill's hostility then towards Ireland. Churchill alleged that Irish neutrality was 'perpetuating partition' and 'alienating' British public opinion.

18 Broadcast by Churchill on 13 May 1945 in *The Times*, 14 May 1945.

19 *Irish Press*, 16 May '45.

20 Maffey to Dominions Office, 21 May '45, in Do 35/1229/WX110/3.

21 *Parl. Deb. (C)*, XXVI, 16 November 1943, col. 2090.

22 *Brooke Diary*, 7 November 1945; Bowman, *op.cit.*, pp 267, 268; *Belfast News Letter*, 8 November 1945.

23 *Brooke Diary*, 24 June '45.

24 *Irish Times*, 18 April 1941.

25 Note by Walshe, 21 April 1941, in NAD, D/FA A2.

26 Memorandum, initialled 'R.F.' on Raid on Belfast, 15-16 April 1941 in NAD, D/T S 14993. The time was probably about 4.35am - see Barton, *Blitz, op.cit.*, pp 128, 129.

27 *Ibid.*, Rudmore Bowen to de Valera, 5 May 1941.

28 Record of transmissions by Hamburg Radio, 13-14 September 1939, in NAD, D/T S 12109.

29 Note by Walshe, 17 April 1941, in NAD, D/T S 14993.

30 Cabinet Conclusions, 16 April '41, in PRONI, CAB 4/469; *Brooke Diary*, 16 April 1941.

31 Barton, *The Blitz, op.cit.*, p 290.

32 Text in NAD, D/T, S14993; see also de Valera to Churchill, 25 May '41, NAD, D/FA P 70, where he states, 'these people, Catholic and Protestant, are our people'.

33 *Irish Times*, 17 April 1941.

34 Maffey to Walshe, 29 March 1941, in NAD, D/FA A2.

35 Report by M.J. Deary, dated 16 July 1941, NAD, D/FA A29.

36 Report in J. J. O'Connell Papers, NLI, Ms 22152.

37 Note of conversation, between Walshe and Hempel, 22 November 1941, in NAD, D/FA A2.

38 *Brooke Diary*, 15 May 1940.

39 *Fin Diary*, 26 April 1941.

40 *Ibid.*, 11 December 1940.

41 U.S. Note to Walshe, 21 February 1944, in NAD, D/FA A53.

42 Reynolds, *Rich Relations, op.cit.*, p 118.

43 Warnock to Morrison, 9 November 1944, in PRONI, CAB 4/605.

44 *Brooke Diary*, 20 April 1942.

45 Canavan, *Frontier Town, op.cit.*, p 210.

46 Mass Observation Archive, *op.cit.*, FR 1309.

47 Memoranda by Finance and Commerce, 4, 12 November 1942, in NAD, D/T S1582.

48 Walshe to Hempel, 15 December 1943, in NAD, D/FA A2.

49 NAD, D/FA A53 *passim.*

50 J.P. Duggan, *Neutral Ireland and the Third Reich* (Dublin, 1985), pp 177-178, 237.

51 Gray to MacRory, 7 October 1942, in Hayes Papers, NLI, Ms 22984.

52 *Ibid.*, Goertz file in Hayes Papers; also NAD, D/FA P 60, memorandum, dated 25 August 1942.

53 De Valera to Churchhill, 25 May '41, NAD, D/FA P70 and *passim.*

54 *The Times*, 28 January 1942; NAD, D/FA P 43/1, 2, 3 *passim.*

55 *Eire and the War; Mr de Valera's Anti-British Record, op.cit.*; Garda report, dated 28 February 1942, in NAD D/FA P 43.

56 *Brooke Diary*, 24 July '45.

57 *Eire and the War; Mr De Valera's Anti-British Record, op.cit.*

58 *Brooke Diary*, 11 July 1940, 4 May 1945.

59 Barclay, *53 (Welsh) Division*, op.cit., p 37.

60 *Irish Times*, 18 April 1941.

61 Barton, *The Blitz, op.cit.*, pp 264-283.

62 *Sunday News*, 28 January 1968; *Brooke Diary*, 3 November; 6,15 December 1940.

63 Fisk, *op.cit.*, p 399.

64 Mass Observation Archive, *op.cit.*, FR1309.

65 Minute, dated 22 April '41, by J Walshe in NAD, D/FA A2.

66 McCusker, *op.cit.*, pp 10, 12.

67 Livingstone, *op.cit.*, p 341.

68 Diary of William McCready, Linen Hall Library, Belfast; see also *William McCready of Whiteabbey, 1909-1982; Diarist and Book Collector* (Belfast, 1985), *passim.*

69 *Woodside Diary*, 30 March, 16 August 1940.

70 Brian Moore, *The Emperor of Ice Cream* (London, 1970), p 28.

71 Doherty, *op.cit.*, p 181.

72 *Sunday News*, 4 February 1968

73 Garda reports, 9, 18 November 1940, in NAD, D/FA A23. See also reference to letter to Hempel from Belfast 'which had all the appearance of a trap laid for him', according to Walshe, in NAD, D/FA P 3, (9 August 1940).

74 *Irish Independent*, 23 May 1941, also NAD, D/FA P 70, *passim.*

75 Walker, *op.cit.*, p 121.

76 John Oliver, *Working at Stormont* (Dublin, 1978), p 68.

77 West, *op.cit.*, p 312.

78 Mass Observation Archive, *op.cit.*, FR 1306.

79 Reynolds, *op.cit.*, p 194

80 Mass Observation Archive, *op.cit.*, FR 1306.

81 Gray to MacRory, 7 October 1942, in Hayes Papers, NLI, Ms 22982.

82 Reynolds, *op.cit.*, pp 119, 257.

83 Cabinet Conclusions, 9 November 1944, PRONI, CAB 4/605.

84 Minutes of Ulster Unionist Party Standing Committee, 11 April, 10 November 1944, 9 February 1945, in PRONI, D1327/7.

85 *Fin Diary*, 30 March 1943.

86 *Woodside Diary*, 14 March 1940, 27 August 1941.

87 *Ibid.*, 10 March 1940, 17 January 1941.

88 *Fin Diary*, 16 March, 10, 11 September 1944.

89 McCusker, *op.cit.*, pp 12, 14.

90 Doherty, *op.cit.*, p 52.

91 Barclay, *op.cit.*, p 37.

92 *Woodside Diary*, 31 March, 16 August, 20 November 1940.

93 Fisk, *op.cit.*, pp 326, 342, 454; *Belfast News Letter*, 3 September 1942.

94 *Brooke Diary*, 3 July 1945.

95 *Sunday News*, 4 February 1968; Walker, *op.cit.*, p 151.

96 Minutes of Ulster Unionist Council Executive Committee, 23 May 1950, in PRONI, D1327/6.

97 J.N. Whyte, 'How much discrimination was there under the Unionist regime, 1921-68?' in T. Gallagher and J. O'Connell, *Contemporary Irish Studies* (Manchester, 1983), p 19.

98 T. Wilson, *Ulster: Conflict and Consent* (Oxford, 1989), pp 126, 7. D.P. Barrett and C.F. Carter, *The Northern Ireland Problem; A Study in Group Relations* (London, 1962), p 112.

99 Cabinet Conclusions, 12 October 1944, PRONI, CAB 4/601.

100 Shea, *op.cit.*, pp 161, 179.

101 D. H. Akenson, *Education & Enmity: the Control of Schooling in Northern Ireland, 1920-50* (Newtown Abbot, 1973), p 180.

102 *Brooke Diary*, 11 July 1944; Cabinet Conclusions, 28 June, 15 October 1945, PRONI, CAB 4/628, 650.

103 *Brooke Diary*, 5 September 1944.

104 Cabinet Conclusions, 15 September 1944, PRONI, CAB 4/597.

105 *Brooke Diary*, 11 July 1944.

106 Cabinet Conclusions, 15 February 1945, PRONI, CAB 4/615; also CAB 4/592, 606, 614, *passim*.

107 Barton, *The Blitz*, *op.cit.*, chapter 7, *passim*; Brodie, *op.cit.*, p 92, chapter 9, *passim*; Blake, *op.cit.*, chapt.12 *passim*.

108 *Brooke Diary*, 18 October 1944.

109 *Belfast News Letter*, 4 January 1945.

110 *Daily Mail*, 19 December 1944.

111 Garda Report, 14 January 1945, also note of Walshe's conversations with Maffey, 16 January 1945 in NAD, D/FA A67.

112 Blake, *op.cit.*, p.528, chapt. 12, *passim*. Major General Peret 'Commander of the Belgium forces', wrote to the then Governor, Lord Granville, 14 December 1945, 'The Belgians, usually stay-at-home, and not accustomed to leaving their native land, came to Ireland with some apprehension... All of us... were deeply impressed by the admirable spirit of ... your own gallant Ulster,' in Maureen Van Tiggelan Papers, in possession of the author.

CHAPTER 7

1 *Northern Whig*, 2 May 1945.

2 *Belfast News Letter*, 8 May 1945.

3 Interview with Malcolm Brodie, 16 March 1995; *Belfast News Letter*, 9 May 1945.

4 *Ibid.*, 9 May 1945.

5 Notes of air raids, by William Ward, 9 May 1945 PRONI, D2742/1.

6 McCready, *op.cit.*, p 16.

7 Barton, *The Blitz*, p 296.

8 Haines, *op.cit.*, p 217, n70.

9 McCusker, *op.cit.*, p 146

10 Doherty, *op.cit.*, pp 79-81.

11 Mullen and Francis, *op.cit.*, p 17.

12 *Brooke Diary*, 7 May '45; *The War Years; Derry 1939-45, op.cit.*, p 53.

13 *Brooke Diary*, 8 May 1945.

14 S. Elliot, *Northern Ireland Parliamentary Election Results, 1921-'72* (Chichester, 1973), *passim*.

15 *Brooke Diary*, 28 July, 13 November 1945; Cabinet Conclusions, 29 November 1945, PRONI,. CAB 4/645.

16 A. Kelly to R. Gransden, 2 April 1946, PRONI, CAB 9J/53.

17 B. Barton, 'Relations between Westminster and Stormont during the Attlee Premiership' in *Irish Political Studies*, vol. 7, pp 1-21.

18 Harkness, *op.cit.*, p 120.

19 See minute, 5 May 1949, in PRO, DO 35/3973.

20 Memorandum by Addison, dated 18 October 1946, in PRO, Premier 8/1222.

21 Memorandrum by Brooke, dated 15 September 1946 in PRONI, CAB 9J/53

22 *Dail Eireann Debates*, Vol. CIX, cols. 2-6.

23 Memorandum by Maginess, 5 August 1951, in PRONI, CAB 9J/53.

24 Report by official working party of officials, dated 1 January 1949 in PRO, CAB 21/1842; also PRO Premier 8/14664, 1222, *passim.*

25 Memorandum by Rugby, dated 17 November 1948, in PRO, CAB 21/1843. Sir John Maffey was created Lord Rugby in 1947.

BIBLIOGRAPHY

MANUSCRIPT SOURCES

A Northern Ireland

1. PUBLIC RECORD OFFICE OF NORTHERN IRELAND, BELFAST
Cabinet papers; CAB 3,4,9 CD
Ministry of Commerce files; COM 61
Ministry of Development files; DEV 9
Ministry of Finance files; FIN 17,18
Ministry of Home Affairs and Public Security Civil Defence files; HA 6
Ministry of Public Security files; HA 18
Information Service (photographs); INF 7

Private papers;
Sir Wilfrid Spender Financial Diary (Sep. 1939-June 1944); D 715
Lord Craigavon Papers; D 1415
Emma Duffin Diary; D 2109
Sir Douglas Harkness Papers; (uncatalogued)
St. Ninian's Church of Ireland Church; notes by the caretaker, William Ward; D 2742
Sir Basil Brooke Diaries; D 3004
Ulster Unionist Party Papers; D 1327

2. LANGFORD LODGE WARTIME CENTRE
Photographs and Archives

3. LINEN HALL LIBRARY, BELFAST
Diary of William McCready

4. QUEEN'S UNIVERSITY, BELFAST
R.M. Henry Collection

5. IN AUTHOR'S POSSESSION
Van Tiggelan Papers, relating to Belgian troops in Northern Ireland during 1945

B. Republic of Ireland

1. NATIONAL ARCHIVES, DUBLIN
Cabinet Minutes; G 3
Department of Taoiseach files; D/T
Department of Foreign Affairs files; D/FA
Department of Justice files; D/J

2. NATIONAL LIBRARY OF IRELAND, DUBLIN
Hayes Papers; Ms 22982,3,4
J.J. O'Connell Papers; Ms 22309

C. Great Britain

1. CHURCHILL COLLEGE, CAMBRIDGE
Churchill Papers

2. IMPERIAL WAR MUSEUM
Material relating to Ireland in World War II, including file on James Magennis, V.C.

3. PUBLIC RECORD OFFICE, LONDON
Cabinet Papers; CAB 21,65,66,123
Home Office files; HO 45
Prime Minister's Office files; Premier 3,4,8
Dominions Office files; DO 35
Foreign Office files; FO 371
Treasury files; T 160

4. TOM HARRISSON MASS OBSERVATION ARCHIVE, UNIVERSITY OF SUSSEX, BRIGHTON
Files relating to Northern Ireland;
Diary of Moya Woodside; MO 5462

PARLIAMENTARY PAPERS

A. United Kingdom
Official Report, 3rd and 5th series, Parliamentary Debates, House of Commons

B. Northern Ireland
Northern Ireland House of Commons Papers
Parliamentary Debates, Official Report, House of Commons

Planning Advisory Committee Report on the general housing problem with particular reference to the clearance of slums, the provision of new housing in the post-war period, 1944.(Cmd. 224, Government of Northern Ireland)

C. Eire
Dail Eireann Parliamentary Debates

156

GOVERNMENT PUBLICATIONS

1 Blake, John W. *Northern Ireland in the Second World War*, (Belfast, 1956)

2. Isles, K.S. and Cuthbert, Norman. *An Economic Survey of Northern Ireland*, (Belfast, 1957)

3. Shearman, Hugh. *Northern Ireland 1921-1971*, (Belfast, 1971)

4. *Ulster Year Book*, (Belfast, 1926-1956)

NEWSPAPERS AND PERIODICALS

Belfast News Letter
Belfast Telegraph
Fermanagh Times
Irish Independent
Irish News
Irish Press
Irish Sword
Irish Times
Londonderry Sentinel
Northern Whig
Stars and Stripes
Sunday News
Sunday Pictorial
Sunday Times
The Times
Volkischer Beobachter

THESES

1. Davidson, Robson. 'The German air-raids on Belfast of April and May 1941 and their consequences', unpublished Ph.D. thesis, Queen's University, Belfast, 1976

2. Harbinson, John F. 'A history of the Northern Ireland Labour Party, 1891-1948', unpublished M.Sc. thesis, Queen's University, Belfast, 1972

INTERVIEWS

1. Malcolm Brodie, 16 March, 1995
2. Lord Brookeborough, 23 February, 1985
3. Sir Douglas Harkness, 4, 11 June, 1979
4. Sir Arthur Kelly, 21, 28 April, 1979
5. Lord J.C. MacDermott, 11, 14 May, 1979
6. James Molyneaux, 20 March, 1995

BOOKS, ARTICLES and PAMPHLETS

Akenson, D.H., *Education and Enmity: The Control of Schooling in Northern Ireland* (Newtown Abbot, 1973)

Barclay, C.N., *The History of the 53rd(Welsh) Division in the Second World War* (London, 1956)

Barrett, D.P., and Carter, C.F., *The Northern Ireland Problem: A Study in Group Relations* (London, 1962)

Barton, Brian, *The Blitz: Belfast in the War Years* (Belfast, 1989)

Barton, Brian, *Brookeborough: The Making of a Prime Minister* (Belfast, 1988)

Barton, Brian, 'Relations between Westminster and Stormont during the Attlee Premiership', *Irish Political Studies*, vol.7

Belfast and Northern Ireland Directory (Belfast, 1921-1948)

Bowman, John, *De Valera and the Ulster Question, 1917-1973* (Oxford, 1982)

Boyd, Marjory, *War Record, Queen's University, Belfast* (Belfast, 1948)

Brodie, Malcolm, *One Hundred Years of Irish Football* (Belfast, 1980)

Brodie, Malcolm, *The Tele: A History of the Belfast Telegraph* (Belfast, 1995)

Buckland, P., *A History of Northern Ireland* (Dublin,1981)

Buckland, P., *The Factory of Grievances: Devolved Government in Northern Ireland, 1921-1939* (Dublin, 1979)

Budge, I., and O'Leary, C., *Belfast: Approach to Crisis: A Study of Belfast Politics 1603-1970* (London, 1973)

Calvocoressi, Peter and Wint, Peter, *Total War: Causes and Courses of the Second World War* (Harmondsworth, 1972)

Canavan, Tony, *Frontier Town: Newry, an Illustrated History* (Belfast, 1989)

Canning, Paul, *British Policy towards Ireland, 1921-1941* (Oxford, 1985)

Carnwath, Dr.Thomas, '*Report to the Special Committee of Belfast Corporation on the Municipal Health Services of the City*' (Belfast, 1941)

Carroll, J.T., *Ireland in the War Years, 1939-1945* (Newton Abbot, 1975)

Carter, Carolle, *The Shamrock and the Swastika: German Espionage in Ireland in World War II* (California, 1977)

Coogan, T.P., *The I.R.A.* (London, 1980)

Ditch, John, *Social Policy in Northern Ireland between 1939-1950* (Avebury, 1988)

Doherty, James, *Post 381; The Memoirs of a Belfast Air Warden* (Belfast, 1989)

Doherty, Richard, *Key to Victory: The Maiden City in the Second World War* (Antrim, 1995)

Donne, Michael, *Pioneers of the Skies: A History of Short Brothers P.L.C.* (Belfast, 1989)

Duggan, J.P., *Neutral Ireland and the Third Reich* (Dublin, 1985)

Dwyer, T.R., *Guests of the Nation: The Story of Allied and Axis Servicemen interned in Ireland during World War II* (Dingle, 1994)

Dwyer, T.R., *Irish Neutrality and the U.S.A., 1939-1947* (Dublin, 1977)

Elliot, S., *Northern Ireland Parliamentary Election Results, 1921-1972* (Chichester, 1973)

Fisk, Robert, *In Time of War: Ireland, Ulster and the Price of Neutrality, 1939-1945* (London, 1983)

Flackes, W.D., *The Enduring Premier* (Belfast, 1962)

Fraser, David, *Alanbrooke* (London, 1982)

Gallagher, T., and O'Connell, J., *Contemporary Irish Studies* (Manchester, 1983)

Gilbert, Martin, *Finest Hour: W,S, Churchill, 1939-1941* (London, 1983)

Harkiness, David, *Northern Ireland since 1920* (Dublin, 1983)

Hawkins, Richard, 'Bending the Beam: Myth and Reality in the bombing of Coventry, Belfast and Dublin', *The Irish Sword*, vol. XIX

Haynes, Keith, *Neither Rogues nor Fools: A History of Campbell College and Campbellians* (Belfast, 1993)

Irish Government, (Department of Defence), *Civilian War Duties*, Public Information Pamphlet No. 1 (Dublin, 1939)

Johnson, David, 'The economic history of Ireland between the wars', *Irish Economic and Social History,* vol.1

Kennedy, Dennis, *The Widening Gulf: Northern Attitudes to the Independent Irish State, 1919-1949* (Belfast, 1988)

Kennedy, L, *The Modernization of Ireland, 1940-1988* (Dublin, 1988)

Keogh, Dermot, *Ireland and Europe, 1919-1989* (Cork, 1989)

Keogh, Dermot, *Twentieth Century Ireland: Nation and State* (Dublin, 1994)

Lacy, Brian, *Siege City: The Story of Derry and Londonderry* (Belfast, 1990)

Lawrence, R.J., *The Government of Northern Ireland: Public Finance and Public Services, 1921-1964* (London, 1965)

Linen Hall Library, Belfast, *William McCready of Whiteabbey, 1909-1982: Diarist and Book Collector* (Belfast, 1985)

Livingstone, Paedar, *The Fermanagh Story* (Enniskillen, 1969)

Longmate, Norman, *The GIs: The American Troops in Britain, 1942-1945* (London, 1975)

McCusker, Breege, *Castle Archdale and Fermanagh in World War II* (Irvinestown, 1993)

MacKenzie, S.P., *The Home Guard: A Military and Political History* (Oxford, 1995)

Maltby, A, *The Government of Northern Ireland, 1922-1972: A Catalogue and Breviate of Parliamentary Papers* (Dublin, 1974)

Mangan, Colm, 'Plans and operations', *The Irish Sword*, vol. XIX

Middlemas, N.L., *British Shipbuilding Yards, Vol. III* (London, 1992)

Moore, Brian, *The Emperor of Ice Cream* (London, 1970)

Moss, Michael and Hume, John, *Shipbuilders to the World: 125 Years of Harland and Wolff* (Belfast, 1986)

Mullen, J., and Francis, D., 'Base One, Londonderry: Derry, the Yanks and World War II', *Ulster Folklife*, vol. 41.

Nolan, K.B., and Williams, T.D., *Ireland in the War Years and After, 1939-1951* (Dublin, 1969)

O'Halpin, Eunan, 'Aspects of Intelligence', *The Irish Sword*, vol. XIX

Oliver, John, *Working at Stormont* (Dublin, 1978)

Open, Michael, *Fading Lights, Silver Screen: A History of Belfast Cinema* (Antrim, 1983)

Oral History Department, Heritage Library, Derry, *The War Years, Derry, 1939-1945* (Derry, 1992)

Parsons, Denis, 'Mobilization and Expansion, 1939-1940', *The Irish Sword*, vol. XIX.

Purdie, Ann, *Molyneaux: The Long View* (Antrim, 1989)

Quinn, John, *Wings over the Foyle* (Belfast, 1995)

Reynolds, David, *Rich Relations: The American Occupation of Britain, 1942-1945* (London, 1995)

Royal Air Force, *Royal Air Force in Northern Ireland: Official V.E. Day Fiftieth Anniversary Souvenir Brochure* (Belfast, 1995)

Shea, Patrick, *Voices and the Sound of Drums: An Irish Autobiography* (Belfast, 1981)

Smith, David J., *Action Stations: Military Airfields of Scotland, the North-East, and Northern Ireland* (Wellingborough, 1985)

Smith, Graham, *When Jim Crow met John Bull* (London, 1987)

Timmins, Nicholas, *The Five Giants: A Biography of the Welfare State* (London, 1995)

Ulster Unionist Council, *Eire and the War: De Valera's Anti-British Record* (Belfast, 1946)

Walker, Graham, *The Politics of Frustration: Harry Midgley and the Failure of Labour in Northern Ireland* (Manchester, 1985)

West, Nigel, *MI 5: British Security Service Operations, 1909-1945* (London, 1981)

Whyte, J.N., 'How much discrimination was there under the Unionist regime, 1921-1968?' in Gallagher T., and O'Connell, J., *Contemporary Irish Studies*, (Manchester, 1983)

Wilson, T, *Ulster: Conflict and Consent* (Oxford, 1989)

Young, Peter, 'Defence and the new Irish State', *The Irish Sword*, vol. XIX

INDEX